In
Search
of
Wagner

V

In Search of Wagner

Theodor Adorno

Translated by

Rodney Livingstone

VERSO

London · New York

Verso gratefully acknowledges the following, whose copyright
translations have been used in citations from Wagner's operas:
The Mastersingers, Tristan and *Rienzi*, EMI; *Lohengrin*, Philips;
Parsifal, Decca; *The Ring*, Deutsche Grammophon.

First published as *Versuch über Wagner*
by Suhrkamp Verlag 1952
This translation first published 1981
This edition published by Verso 1991
© Suhrkamp Verlag 1952, 1974
Translation © New Left Books 1981

Verso
UK: 6 Meard Street, London W1V 3HR
USA: 29 West 35th Street, New York, NY 10001-2291

Verso is the imprint of New Left Books

British Library Cataloguing in Publication Data
Adorno, Theodor W. (Theodor Wiesengrund) *1903-1969*
In search of Wagner.
1. German operas
I. Title II. [Versuch uber Wagner]. *English*
782.1092

ISBN 0-86091-796-7

US Library of Congress Cataloging-in-Publication Data
Adorno, Theodor W., 1903-1969.
[Versuch über Wagner. English]
In search of Wagner / Theodor Adorno.
p.   cm.
Translation of: Versuch über Wagner.
Includes bibliographical references and index.
ISBN 0-86091-796-7 (pbk.)
1. Wagner, Richard, 1813-1883—Criticism and interpretation.
I. Title
[ML410.W1A5953   1991]
782.1′092—dc20

Typeset in Monotype Bembo by Servis Filmsetting Ltd, Manchester
Printed in Great Britain by Biddles Ltd, Guildford.

Contents

Translator's Preface

Sources of quotations from Wagner's operas have been added for the convenience of the reader. Other footnotes are by Adorno except where indicated. Explanatory material introduced into the body of the text by the translator has been placed in square brackets.

The preliminary reading indispensable to the task of translating this book was carried out in Frankfurt with the aid of a grant from the British Academy. I should like to record my gratitude for its generosity. My thanks are due also to Dr Eric Graebner of the Music Department of Southampton University for having given me some much-needed assistance with many problems of musical terminology. Over and above this his expert knowledge of Wagner's scores was invaluable in sorting out some knotty points in the translation itself. I am greatly indebted to him for the scrupulous care with which he answered all my queries. The responsibility for any errors that remain lies, of course, with the present translator.

Rodney Livingstone
Southampton, July 1980

for GRETEL

Horses are the survivors
of the age of heroes.

Preface

In Search of Wagner was written between autumn 1937 and spring 1938 in London and New York. It is intimately bound up with Max Horkheimer's essay 'Egoism and the Movement for Emancipation: towards an anthropology of the bourgeois era', which appeared in 1936, as well as with other writings emanating from the Institute for Social Research during those years. The work was first published as a whole by Suhrkamp in 1952.

Four chapters, the first, second and the last two, had already appeared in numbers 1 and 2 of the *Zeitschrift für Sozialforschung*. Most of this edition was destroyed during the German occupation of France; only a very few copies have survived. The author did not think it proper when preparing the book for publication to make any significant emendations to the original wording of the chapters already printed. He felt rather less constrained in his treatment of some of the unpublished chapters; he has felt free to incorporate something of his subsequent ideas. On the other hand, almost no notice has been taken of the secondary literature on Wagner that has since appeared. In this respect the correspondence with King Ludwig and the two final volumes of Ernest Newman's monumental biography contain important new material for an assessment of Wagner's social character. The present writer feels justified in regarding them as providing confirmation of what he has said here on the subject.

The paperback edition corrects printing errors but apart from these there are only a few minor changes. The author's more recent views on Wagner would not have fitted into the framework of the present study. His essay 'The Score of Parsifal' is to be found in the *Moments Musicaux*; the talk on 'The Relevance of Wagner Today', which was given during the Berlin Festival in September 1963, has not yet appeared in print.

The Author
December 1963

Social Character

Das Liebesverbot, the first of Wagner's operas performed in his lifetime, makes use of a libretto whose subject-matter was taken from Shakespeare's *Measure for Measure*, with the difference that, in Wagner's own words, 'the hypocrite was brought to book solely by the avenging power of love itself', instead of being unmasked by a political authority. To the twenty-one-year-old composer, or so it seemed to the older man looking back on his youth, Shakespeare's comedy appeared as coloured by the imaginative worlds of *Ardinghello* and *Das junge Europa*.[1] 'The ground-note of my interpretation was directed against puritanical hypocrisy and hence led to the bold celebration of "free sensuality". I strove to view the serious Shakespearean subject in this light alone; I saw only the grim, morally austere regent, aflame with a consuming passion for the beautiful novice'—and he reproaches himself for the Feuerbachian mood of the early work, which caused him to overlook the element of dramatic 'justice' that alone made possible the development of the opposing forces in Shakespeare. After the fiasco of the provincial premiere, the work fell immediately into total oblivion, and even when Wagner became famous the zeal of the philologists was unable to recall it to life. In his next opera, the

---

[1] *Ardinghello*, a novel by Wilhelm Heinse, published in 1787, was widely read for its frank praise of the pagan sensuality of Classical Greece. *Das junge Europa* was a three-part novel by Heinrich Laube that appeared between 1833 and 1837. It expresses both the initial revolutionary aspirations of Laube (and the Young German movement) as well as his subsequent disappointment and resigned acceptance of the existing social order in Germany coupled with vague hopes of a better future. *Translator's note.*

workings of justice showed themselves more tolerant of hypocrisy: *Rienzi* not only became Wagner's first success, making his name and giving him a position; until recently it filled the opera houses with its clamour even though its Meyerbeerian stance is as completely incompatible with the norms of Wagnerian music drama as the novice of Palermo had been.[2] Of course, as early as the opening scene Wagner abandons his previous celebration of free sensuality. Instead he denounces it. A gang of young noblemen is shown in the act of attempting an assault on the virtue of the chaste Irene. She is blindly devoted to her brother Rienzi, the last Roman tribune and the first bourgeois terrorist. With complete fidelity to his source, but also with approval, Wagner reveals the truth about Rienzi's 'liberation movement':

> Freedom I proclaim for the sons of Rome!
> Yet let everyone by no unseemly conduct [*Raserei*],
> Show that he is a Roman!
> Bid this day welcome
> That it may avenge you and your shame. (Act I, sc. 1)

After this, 'unseemly conduct' can exist only when permitted: as a morally sanctioned vengeance. But when Adriano Colonna, the vacillating representative of feudal power, addresses Rienzi as 'the bloodstained minion of liberty' for taking such vengeance, he fails to perceive that his own class is the prime beneficiary of the embargo on unseemly conduct. Rienzi bows down to him with the words:

> I always knew you to be noble;
> The just man has no cause to loath you. (Act I, sc. 2)

and a stage-direction of Wagner's notes admiringly: 'the Peace Envoys are youths drawn from the best Roman families. They are dressed, half in ancient fashion, in white silk robes, with garlands in their hair and carrying silver staves in their hands.'[3] The best

---

[2] *The Novice of Palermo* was the title substituted for *Das Liebesverbot* (Love Prohibited) in order to placate the censor. *Translator's note.*

[3] Act II, sc. 1

families belong to the national community:

> My mind did not conceive its bold plan
> For the destruction of your class.
> I want only to create the law
> To which nobles and people alike will defer. (Act i, sc. 2)

Nominally, the oppressed too are received into this community:

> Well, I shall make Rome great and free
> I shall awaken it from its slumber
> And the man you see in the dust
> I shall make into a free Roman citizen. (Ibid.)

If the 'hero of liberty' lets the feudal lords see that he has no intention of doing them serious harm, he redresses the balance by restricting the claims of the oppressed to consciousness alone:

> . . . to bring light to those whose thoughts were lowly,
> To raise up what had fallen into the dust.
> You transformed the people's shame
> Into greatness, splendour and majesty.[4]

In short, the Roman insurrection is directed against the libertine style of life and not against the class enemy, and it is only logical, if naive, that the resounding political action should be initiated by Adriano's private family quarrels. From the very outset Rienzi's revolution aims at integration: when he hears the slogans of the conflicting parties—'for Colonna!', 'for Orsini!'—the motto that he, as the prophet of a totalitarian ideology, hurls back is 'for Rome!'. As the first servant of the greater social totality, the dictator Rienzi spurns the title of king, just as Lohengrin will later refuse the rank of duke. In exchange of course he is as happy to accept the laurels of victory in advance as he is to bestow them on others. Another stage direction, likewise in conformity with the categories of egoism and the movement for emancipation, states:[5]

[4] Act V, sc. i. This is taken from Rienzi's own soliloquy. *Translator's note.*
[5] Cf. Max Horkheimer, 'Egoism and the Movement for Emancipation', in the *Zeitschrift für Sozialforschung*, 5 (1936), p. 161 ff.

'Enter Rienzi as a Tribune, wearing outrageous and ostentatious robes.'[6] Within this historical costume-play we almost perceive some glimmering realization that the true nature of the hero lies in his self-knowledge. Self-praise and pomp—features of Wagner's entire output and the emblems of Fascism—spring from the presentiment of the transient nature of bourgeois terrorism, of the death instinct implicit in the heroism that proclaims itself. The man who seeks immortality during his lifetime doubts that his achievement will survive him and so he celebrates his own obsequies with festive ceremonial. Behind Wagner's facade of liberty, death and destruction stand waiting in the wings: the historic ruins that come crashing down on the heads of the defeated Gods and the guilt-laden world of the *Ring*.

Wagner's own view of himself in later years was that 'the works of his more mature artistic development' achieved a 'harmony between the two tendencies' of his early period, namely unrestrained sexuality and an ideal of asceticism. But this harmony is achieved in the name of death. Pleasure and death become one: Brünnhilde abandons herself at the end of Act III to her beloved Siegfried for 'a laughing death', at the moment when she means to awaken and return to life, and Isolde, too, experiences her corporeal death as the 'highest bliss'. Even where, as in Tannhäuser, the opposition between sexuality and asceticism is an explicit theme, their reconciliation is achieved at the moment of death. His hostility towards 'puritanical hypocrisy' is by no means spent. The knights who have welcomed the renegade Tannhäuser back into their circle of virtue against his will, now want him killed because their moral sense has been outraged by his having learnt 'on the extreme left' what their middle-to-upper-class world forbids them to know. And the crowd rewards them with the 'tumultuous applause' of the Rienzi-national community, which in this instance the work fails to endorse. The saintly Elizabeth is to a certain extent in sympathy with the defiant hedonist. This proves her worth since she dies in opposition to the order from which she protects him. Asceticism and rebellion join forces against the norm. Henceforth, knights, guild-masters and all figures from the

[6] Act II, sc. 1.

middle of the social hierarchy are given a bad press by Wagner: Hunding, the primordial husband, is dispatched to the Lower World without much ceremony. But the contemptuous wave of the hand with which Wotan dismisses Hunding is itself essentially a terrorist gesture. Such defamations of the bourgeois, who is after all quick enough to celebrate his own resurrection in *The Mastersingers*, serve the same purpose as in the age of totalitarianism. It is not the case that he is to be succeeded by a different human ideal. All that is intended is a dispensation from middle-class obligations. The insignificant are punished, while the prominent go scot-free. This at any rate is what happens in the *Ring*. It is true that Wotan appears to defend rebellion, but he does so only in the interests of his universal imperialist design and in terms of the categories of freedom of action ('No written treaty of trust bound you, villain, to me') and breach of contract ('For wherever forces stir boldly, there I frankly counsel war').[7] The sovereign God leaves his protégé in the lurch and cannot think of a better way to extricate himself from his political contradictions than by abruptly breaking off the discussion with his adviser [Brünnhilde] and punishing her ruthlessly when she carries out his original plan, only to end up taking leave of her with fatherly sentimentality.

According to Newman, Wagner expressed his abhorrence of a photograph of himself from his first period in Paris with the words: 'It made me look like a sentimental Marat.'[8] Virtue sentimentally reflects the terror it spreads. This sentimentality assumes sinister features in Wagner's make-up: those of the man who begs for sympathy. It is not for nothing that he, unlike the sons of parsons and officials of the generation before him, came from the Bohemian milieu of dilettantish artists which was then new to Germany; it is not for nothing that the period of his rise to fame coincided with that economically precarious age in which opera had ceased to enjoy the security of courtly patronage but had not yet acquired the protection of civil law and regular royalties.[9] In a professional world in which a successful composer like

[7] *Siegfried*, Act II, sc. 1 and *Valkyrie*, Act II, sc. 1.
[8] Ernest Newman, *The Life of Richard Wagner*, Vol. 1, London 1933, p. 18.
[9] Cf. Newman, Vol. 1, p. 135 ff. and especially p. 137.

Lortzing could starve to death, it was essential for Wagner to excel by developing the virtuosity that enabled him to achieve bourgeois goals at the cost of his bourgeois integrity. Only a few weeks after he had fled from Dresden, following his prominent involvement in Bakunin's uprising, he wrote to Liszt requesting that he obtain a salary for him from the Grand Duchess of Weimar, the Duke of Coburg and the Princess of Prussia.[10] It would be as impertinent to express indignation at Wagner's lack of character as to deny that it leads deeply into the centre of his work. It is represented there by Siegmund. As a restless wanderer he appeals for sympathy and uses this as a means of acquiring a woman and a weapon. In the process he makes use of moralistic turns of speech: he claims to have fought on behalf of persecuted innocence and a love that had been thwarted. He is thus a revolutionary who conciliates the despised members of the middle class by recounting heroic deeds now past. What is decisive here is not the deceit, the posturing. His crime is not that he is a deceiver, but that by appealing for sympathy he confers recognition on the ruling classes and identifies himself with them. A lack of restraint in begging could suggest a particular independence of bourgeois norms. But here it has the opposite meaning. The power of the existing order over the protester is so great that he is no longer capable of separating himself from it or even of putting up any genuine resistance: and in the same way there is an absence of tension in Wagner's harmony as it descends from the leading note and sinks from the dominant into the tonic. It is the fawning stance of the mother's boy who talks himself and others into believing that his kind parents can deny him nothing, for the very purpose of making sure that they don't. The shock of the first few weeks in emigration brought Wagner very close to this state of mind. On 5 June 1849, the 36-year-old composer who had completed *Lohengrin* and was already at work on the *Ring*, wrote to Liszt: 'Like a spoiled child of my homeland I exclaim: "Were I only home again in a little house by the wood and might leave the devil to look after this great world which at the best I should not even

[10] Cf. *Correspondence of Wagner and Liszt*, Vol. 1, translated by Francis Heffer, New York 1969, p. 29.

care to conquer, because its possession would be even more loathsome than is its mere aspect."'[11] And in the same letter he added: 'Often I bleat like a calf for its stable and for the udder of its life-giving mother . . . With all my courage I am often the most miserable coward! Despite your magnanimous offers I frequently consider with a deadly terror the shrinking of my cash.'[12] The power of the bourgeoisie over Wagner is so absolute that as a bourgeois he finds himself unable to satisfy the requirements of bourgeois respectability. The appeal for sympathy provides a specious resolution of the conflict of interests by enabling the victim to identify with the cause of his oppressor: even in Wagner's official revolutionary writings the king plays a positive role. In his role of beggar, Wagner violates the taboos of the bourgeois work-ethic, but his blessing redounds to the glory of his benefactors. He is an early example of the changing function of the bourgeois category of the individual. In his hopeless struggle with the power of society, the individual seeks to avert his own destruction by identifying with that power and then rationalizing the change of direction as authentic individual fulfilment. The impotent petitioner becomes the tragic panegyrist. In a later historical period these features acquired the greatest significance, when tyrants took to threats of suicide in a crisis, suffered paroxysms of weeping in public and imparted a whining note to their voices. For the focal points of decay in the bourgeois character, in terms of its own morality, are the prototypes of its subsequent transformation in the age of totalitarianism.

Even in later years Wagner exhibits this configuration of envy, sentimentality and destructiveness. His follower Glasenapp, in a reminiscence of his last stay in Venice, reports that 'at the sight of the numerous closed unknown palaces' he had exclaimed: '"That is property! The source of all corruption! Proudhon had a far too material and external view of it. For considerations of property determine the vast majority of marriages and this in turn is the root cause of racial degeneration."'[13] Here we see the entire syndrome:

[11] Ibid., p. 23.
[12] Ibid., pp. 26–7.
[13] Carl F. Glasenapp, *Das Leben Richard Wagners*, Vol. 6, Leipzig 1911, p. 764.

the insight into the senselessness of the ruling property arrangements is diverted into a fury about pleasure-seeking, is de-
politicized in the phrase 'far too external', and obscured by the
substitution of biological concepts for social ones. In his Bayreuth
phase Wagner's personality assumes a dictatorial demeanour.
Once again the unimpeachable Glasenapp is a reliable witness: 'Yet
a further feature was drawn to our attention, one which was not
just characteristic of this final period of his life. It was not possible
to keep anything hidden from him; he always knew everything.
When Mrs Wagner wanted to give him a surprise of any sort, it
would turn out that he had dreamt about it the previous night and
told her in the morning.' In short, as the German idiom runs: he
spits in your soup. Glasenapp continues: 'This ability to see
through people often appeared demonic, particularly with
strangers: his penetrating gaze would enable him to discern a
person's foibles at a glance and it often happened that, even though
he had no wish to offend a person, he nevertheless touched on the
sorest points.'[14]

This tendency was particularly marked in Wagner's treatment
of the Jewish conductor of *Parsifal*. Liberal enthusiasts frequently
make use of the friendship with Hermann Levi to prove the
harmlessness of Wagner's anti-Semitism. Glasenapp's chronicle,
written with the intention of emphasizing Wagner's philanthropic
and broadminded nature, involuntarily gives the game away. On
June 18, 1881, Levi arrived ten minutes late for luncheon at
Wahnfried. Wagner rebuked him with the words: 'You are ten
minutes late: impunctuality is second only to disloyalty', and even
before they sat down to eat, he handed Levi an anonymous letter
begging him not to allow *Parsifal* to be conducted by a Jew. At the
table Levi sat silent; when Wagner asked him why he was so quiet,
Levi, from his own account, replied that he could not understand
why Wagner had not simply torn up the letter. Wagner's answer,
also reported by Levi, was: 'I'll tell you why . . . If I had not shown
the letter to anyone and destroyed it, then some of its contents
might have continued to influence me. But as it is, I can assure you
that I shall not retain even the slightest memory of it.' Without

[14] Ibid., p. 771

taking leave, Levi went to Bamberg and from there sent Wagner an urgent request to be relieved of his post as conductor of *Parsifal*. Wagner telegraphed back: 'Friend, you are most earnestly requested to return to us quickly; the principal bone of contention can easily be removed.' Levi insisted on his resignation, whereupon he received a letter containing these sentences: 'My dear, best friend. All honour to your feelings, but you certainly do not make things easy for yourself or for us! Your habit of gloomy introspection is something that could cast a shadow over our relationship! We are unanimous in our view that the whole world should be told about this shit, and for this it is essential that you do not run away from us and give people cause to think the wrong thing. For God's sake come back to us and at long last come to know us for what we are! Hold fast to your faith, but take a good measure of courage as well!—Perhaps—this will turn out to be a turning point in your life—But at all events—you are my *Parsifal* conductor.'[15]

The sadistic desire to humiliate, sentimental conciliatoriness and above all the wish to bind the maltreated Levi to him emotionally—all these elements enter into Wagner's casuistry: it is indeed demonic, but in another sense than Glasenapp's. Every soothing word is accompanied by a new sting. It is the same kind of demonism that Wagner himself has in mind in his autobiography when he recalls the scene when, although not yet fully matriculated, he joined a horde of students in a raid on two Leipzig brothels. Even in his later account of the affair he is not fully able to throw off the moralistic veil that had been used to cloak this purge: 'I do not believe that the ostensible motive for this outrage, which, it is true, was to be found in a fact that was a grave menace to public morality, had any weight with me whatever; on the contrary, it was the purely devilish fury of these popular outbursts that drew me, too, like a madman into their vortex.'[16]

If as victim Wagner asks for sympathy and so goes over to the

[15] Ibid., pp. 500–02.

[16] R. Wagner, *My Life*, London 1911, p. 49; and cf. Newman, Vol. 1, p. 87. The pretext for the assault was the fury directed against 'a hated magistrate who, it was rumoured, had unlawfully taken under his protection a house of ill-fame in that quarter'. *Translator's note*.

rulers, he is nevertheless inclined to despise other victims. His game of cat-and-mouse with Levi has its parallels in his works. Wotan has a bet with Mime for Mime's own head, but without the latter's cooperation and against his will: the dwarf is at the mercy of the God just as the guest was at the mercy of his host in Wahnfried. The entire *Siegfried* action hinges on this event, since the only reason why Mime strives for Siegfried's death is that Wotan has pledged to Siegfried the head Mime had thus forfeited.[17] Insult is added to injury: this is Wagner's way above all with the lower beings. Alberich who 'scratches his head' is scorned by the nature sprites he lusts after as a 'swarthy, scaly sulphurous dwarf'. In Nibelheim Wotan and Loge make fun of Mime's sufferings.[18] Siegfried torments the dwarf because he 'cannot stand him',[19] without his aura of lofty nobility preventing him from deriving satisfaction from someone else's impotence. The ridicule of Magdalene, the old maid [in *The Mastersingers*], is the obverse of the cult of purity. Beckmesser too is a victim: in order to gain bourgeois respectability and the wealthy bride, he is forced to take part in the unbourgeois masquerade, the feudal charade of serenades and song contest whose image is as necessary to the bourgeoisie as is their readiness wantonly to destroy it. Klingsor, the Alberich of the Christian cosmos is derided by Kundry with the question, 'Are you chaste?', and the knights of the Grail are at one with the Rose of Hell [Kundry] in mocking him:

> The hand of violence he laid upon himself
> Then turned toward the Grail—
> The Guardian drove him off with scorn. (Act I)

Titurel treats the penitent who castrated himself just as the Pope had treated Tannhäuser.[20] But in the mature Wagner there is no authority to annul that verdict.

[17] Cf. 'From today ward your wise head well: / I leave it forfeit to him / Who has never learnt fear!' (i.e. Siegried), *Siegfried*, Act I, sc. 2. *Translator's note*.

[18] Cf. *Rhinegold*, sc. 3, where Alberich, who has gained possession of the Ring and the Tarnhelm, lords it over Mime and forces him to work for him. *Translator's note*.

[19] *Siegfried*, Act I, sc. 1, where Siegfried sets the bear on Mime. *Translator's note*.

[20] He damns him to all eternity. (Act III, sc. 3.) *Translator's note*.

Instead we have Wagner's sense of humour. His villains are turned into comic figures by means of the denunciation they are subjected to: misshapen dwarfs like Alberich and Mime, a maltreated bachelor like Beckmesser. Wagner's humour metes out cruel treatment. He revives the half-forgotten humour of the early bourgeois who once upon a time had inherited the devil's grin, but now remains frozen ambiguously between pity and damnation. Malvolio and Shylock are his theatrical forebears. It is not simply that the poor devil is ridiculed; in the excitement caused by the laughter at his expense the memory of the injustice that he has suffered is obliterated. The use of laughter to suspend justice is debased into a charter for injustice. When Wotan dupes the giants who had been promised Freia in the contract, he does so by pretending that the contract had all been a joke:

> How cunning to take in earnest
> what was agreed only in jest! (*Rhinegold*, sc. 2)

The insistence that something is all a joke is a time-honoured device for rationalizing the worst. Wagner finds precedents for this in the fairy-tales of the German tradition. None is more apposite than the story of the Jew in the bramble-bush. 'Now as the Jew stood there caught in the bramble-bush, the worthy lad was overcome by a mischievous idea: he took up his fiddle and began to play it. At once the Jew's feet started to twitch and he began to leap about; and the more the lad played, the better the Jew danced.' Wagner's music, too, is a worthy lad that treats the villains in like manner, and the comedy of their suffering not only gives pleasure to whoever inflicts it; it also stifles any questions about its justification and tacitly presents itself as the ultimate authority. In his personal relationships, this aspect of Wagner's sense of humour repelled both Liszt and Nietzsche. He himself provides evidence of this: 'Wagner said to Nietzsche's sister: "Your brother is just like Liszt; he doesn't like my jokes either."'[21] When once, in a scene that has become notorious, Wagner fell into a rage with Nietzsche and the latter remained silent, Wagner remarked that Nietzsche, so refined were his manners, would certainly go far in life; he,

[21] Kurt Hildebrandt, *Wagner und Nietzsche*, Breslau 1924, p. 291.

Wagner, had felt the absence of this all his life. This is the sort of witticism that puts its object completely in the wrong and allows of no reply; it deforms sensitivity into pushiness and transfigures coarseness, presenting it as the vitality of genius. But even worse, the darkest secret of Wagner's humour is that it turns not only against his victims, but also against himself. The premature suspension of justice by laughter is too dearly purchased: the clock strikes and the laughing grimace is frozen. It is not the healthy cynicism of the man who confronts us with the frailty of creation, by reminding man of his animal nature, but the destructive cynicism of the person who feels that the unity of nature lies in the fact that all, man and animal, victim and judge, deserve their downfall, and who, grinning, legitimates the downfall of the victim by pointing to his own moral annihilation. Hildebrandt, who owes his mistrust of humour to the school of Stefan George,[22] regarded Wagner's habit of cynical self-denigration as the real cause of his quarrel with Nietzsche. 'Yet there was one particular remark which cut Nietzsche to the quick. The conversation'—it was during the last sojourn of Nietzsche and Wagner in Sorrento—'had turned to the poor attendance at the Bayreuth Festival. Nietzsche's sister reports that Wagner had once observed angrily, "The Germans no longer wished to have anything to do with heathen Gods and heroes; what they wanted to see was something Christian".'[23] As important as the question whether there really was a connection between the production of *Parsifal* and the economic interest of the founder of Bayreuth, is his gesture of self-immolation: not only does he beg shamelessly; he is also prepared to accuse himself of fraud and so plays almost wilfully into Nietzsche's hands. The author of *Parsifal* admits to being Klingsor and the slogan 'Redemption for the Redeemer' takes on unpleasant connotations. Of course, it is an open question whether any of this could be a cause of much rejoicing to Nietzsche, let alone the George school. By betraying the happiness of his own dream—and his work is constantly on the look-out for betrayal—

[22] Stefan George (1868–1933), the hieratic founder of symbolist poetry in Germany. His school of disciples was influential in poetry and criticism in the first half of the century. *Translator's note.*

[23] Hildebrandt, p. 344.

he momentarily allows his gaze to be deflected from the misery of the world that stands in need of it: 'they want to see something Christian'.

The contradiction between mockery of the victim and self-denigration is also a definition of Wagner's anti-Semitism. The gold-grabbing, invisible, anonymous, exploitative Alberich, the shoulder-shrugging, loquacious Mime, overflowing with self-praise and spite, the impotent intellectual critic Hanslick-Beckmesser[24]—all the rejects of Wagner's works are caricatures of Jews. They stir up the oldest sources of the German hatred of the Jews and, at the same time, the romanticism of *The Mastersingers* seems on occasion to anticipate the abusive verses that were not heard on the streets until sixty years later:

> Noble baptist! Christ's precursor!
> Receive us graciously
> There at the River Jordan.[25]

Wagner's anti-Semitism is something he shared with other representatives of what Marx called the German Socialism of 1848. But his version advertises itself as a private idiosyncrasy that stubbornly resists all negotiations. It is the basis of Wagnerian humour. Aversion and laughter come together in a clash of words. Siegfried says to Mime:

> when I watch you standing, shuffling and shambling,
> servilely stooping, squinting and blinking,
> I long to seize you by your nodding neck
> and make an end of your obscene blinking!

And shortly after:

> 'But I can't abide you,
> don't forget that so easily!' (*Siegfried*, Act I, sc. 1)

[24] Beckmesser in *The Mastersingers* was modelled on the critic Eduard Hanslick (1825–1904), a fierce opponent of Wagner and an ardent partisan of Brahms. *Translator's note.*

[25] Act I, sc. 1.

This is reminiscent of the description of Jewish speech in the essay on Judaism and leaves no doubt as to the source of such monstrous beings as Mime and Alberich: 'The first thing that strikes our ear as quite outlandish and unpleasant, in the Jew's production of the voice-sounds, is a creaking, squeaking, buzzing snuffle: add thereto an employment of words in a sense quite foreign to our nation's tongue, and an arbitrary twisting of the structure of our phrases— and this mode of speaking acquires at once the character of an intolerable mumbo-jumbo; so that when we hear this Jewish talk, our attention dwells involuntarily on its repulsive *how*, rather than on any meaning of its intrinsic *what*.'[26] Jewish speech is thereby dismissed.

However, this idiosyncratic hatred is of the type that Benjamin had in mind when he defined disgust as the fear of being thought to be the same as that which is found disgusting. Newman places particular emphasis on the description of Mime in the original version, which Wagner subsequently deleted: 'Mime, the Nibelung, alone. He is small and bent, somewhat deformed and hobbling. His head is abnormally large, his face is dark ashen colour and wrinkled, his eyes small and piercing, with red rims, his grey beard long and scrubby, his head bald and covered with a red cap . . . There must be nothing approaching caricature in all this: his aspect, when he is quiet, must be simply eerie: it is only in moments of extreme excitement that he becomes outwardly ludicrous, but never too uncouth. His voice is husky and harsh, but this again ought of itself never to provoke the listener to laughter.'[27] Wagner's fear of caricature which, after all, in theatrical terms, would not have provided an inappropriate contrast with the serious underworld deity, Alberich, suggests, as does the suppression of this stage direction, that Wagner recoiled with shock from the similarity between Mime and himself. His own physical appearance, disproportionately small, with over-large head and protruding chin, bordered on the abnormal and only fame preserved him from ridicule. The uncontrollable

[26] R. *Wagner's Prose Works*, translated by W.A. Ellis (1893), New York 1966, Vol. 5, p. 71. All quotations from Wagner's prose writings are taken from this edition, sometimes in a slightly adapted form. *Translator's note.*

[27] Newman, Vol. 2, London 1937, p. 321.

loquacity, on which his first wife remarks, could easily be deduced
from his prose works, had it not been documented as thoroughly as
his habit of extravagant gesticulation. He pursues his victims down
to the level of their biological nature because he saw himself as
having only barely escaped being a dwarf. However, the fact that
all the rumours concerning Wagner's own Jewish ancestry can be
traced back, according to Newman's investigations, to that self-
same Nietzsche, who had opposed Wagner's anti-Semitism, is a
phenomenon that has its own logic. Nietzsche knew the secret of
Wagner's idiosyncrasies and broke their spell by naming them.

The realm of idiosyncrasy, usually conceived as the individual
sphere par excellence, is in Wagner's case the realm also of the social
and universal. The impenetrable mystery of his blind intolerance is
rooted in the no less impenetrable mystery of the processes of
society. It is society that has branded the outcast with all the
stigmata that make others turn away in revulsion. Hence to the
man who deserts to the side of the real culprits, social realities must
appear as the work of mysterious conspiracies. One aspect of his
revulsion from Jews is his fantasy of their universal power. In the
essay 'Clarification about Judaism in Music' Wagner ascribes all
forms of resistance to his work to imagined Jewish conspiracies;
whereas in reality his cause was actively promoted by Meyerbeer,
supposedly the chief instigator of these intrigues, until Wagner
himself publicly attacked him. Race theory assumes its rightful
place in the no man's land between idiosyncrasy and paranoia. The
middle-class Wagner needed no lessons on the subject from
Gobineau, the dispossessed feudal seigneur, with whom he was
friendly in his old age. As early as *Siegfried* we can find the words:

> Every thing has its own nature;
> And these you cannot change.
> This spot I cede to you: take a strong stand
> Contend with your brother Mime;
> You may fare better with his kind.
> More than that you will soon learn too![28]

The entire story of the *Ring* is implicated in this. Alberich steals the

[28] *Siegfried*, Act II, sc. 1.

ring and curses love because the Rhine Maidens refuse to surrender to him: the dialectic of instinct and domination is reduced to a difference of 'nature' rather than one socially caused. The absolute distinction drawn in the *Ring* between the different natural kinds becomes the basis of the life and death struggle, its apparent historical structure notwithstanding. If in the social process of life 'ossified relationships' form a second nature, then it is this second nature at which Wagner gazes transfixed, mistaking it for the first. From the outset—in 1850—anti-Semitism is expressed in the categories of nature, above all, those of immediacy and the people, and he already contrasts these categories with 'liberalism': 'When we strove for the emancipation of the Jews, we virtually were more the champions of an abstract principle, than of a concrete case: just as all our liberalism was not a very lucid mental sport— since we went for the freedom of the people without knowledge of the people, nay, with a dislike of any genuine contact with it—so our eagerness to level up the rights of Jews was far rather stimulated by a general idea, than by any real sympathy; for with all our speaking and writing in favour of the Jews' emancipation, we always felt instinctively repelled by any actual, operative contact with them.'[29]

Wagner's anti-Semitism assembles all the ingredients of subsequent varieties. His hatred is so extreme that, if we are to believe Glasenapp, the news of the deaths of 400 Jews in the fire in the *Ringtheater* in Vienna inspired him to make jokes.[30] He had even conceived the notion of the annihilation of the Jews. He differs from his ideological descendants only in that he equates annihilation with salvation. Thus the closing section of the essay on the Jews contains sentences that, however ambivalently, are reminiscent of another tract on the Jewish Question: 'Yet another Jew have we to name, who appeared among us as a writer. From out his isolation as a Jew, he came among us seeking for redemption; he found it not, and had to learn that *only with our redemption, too, into genuine manhood*, would he ever find it. To become man at once with us, however, means firstly for the Jew as much as ceasing to be

[29] R. *Wagner*, Vol. 3, p. 80.
[30] Cf. Glasenapp, Vol. 6, p. 551.

a Jew. And this Börne had done. Yet Börne, of all others, teaches us that this redemption cannot be reached in ease and cold, indifferent and complacence, but costs—as cost it must for us—sweat, anguish, want, and all the dregs of suffering and sorrow. Without once looking back, take your part in this regenerative work of deliverance through self-annulment; then are we one and undissevered! But remember, only one thing can redeem you from the burden of your curse: the redemption of Ahasuerus—*Going under!*'[31] Without any attempt at differentiation we find intertwined here the Marxian idea of the social emancipation of the Jews as the emancipation of society from the profit-motive of which they are the symbolic representatives, and the idea of the destruction of the Jews themselves. And he is not content simply with the disappearance of the hated people itself: 'If our culture is destroyed, that is no great loss; but if it is destroyed by the *Jews*, that would be a disgrace.'[32] The mode of existence that longs for the destruction of the Jew is aware that it is itself beyond redemption. Hence its own downfall is interpreted as the end of the world and Jews are seen as the agents of doom. At its peak, bourgeois nihilism is also the wish to annihiliate the bourgeois. In the sinister realm of Wagner's reactionary outlook we find inscribed letters that his work wrested from his character.

---

[31] Wagner, Vol. 3, p. 100. Ludwig Börne (1786–1837) was a literary and political journalist of the Young German School. His principal work, *Briefe aus Paris*, displays a sharp wit and a satirical talent resembling that of Heine. *Translator's note.*

[32] Glasenapp, Vol. 6, p. 435.

2

Gesture

It would be rewarding to examine the heaps of rubbish, detritus and filth upon which the works of major artists appear to be erected, and to which they still owe something of their character, even though they have just managed to escape by the skin of their teeth. Shadowing Schubert is the figure of the tavern gambler, with Chopin it is the frequenter of *salons*, a type very hard to pin down; with Schumann it is the chromolithograph and with Brahms, the music professor. Their productive energies have asserted themselves cheek by jowl with their parodies, and their greatness lies in the minute distance that separates them from these models from which at the same time they draw collective energies. It is not so easy to discover a model for Wagner. But the chorus of indignation that greeted Thomas Mann when he let fall the word 'dilettante' in connection with Wagner suggests that he touched a raw nerve. 'His relationship to the individual arts from which he composed his "*Gesamtkunstwerk*" is worth pondering; there is something peculiarly dilettantish about it, something upon which Nietzsche has commented in his adulatory "Fourth Observation Out-of-Season", where he says of Wagner's childhood and youth: "His youth was that of a versatile dilettante who will never make good. He was not subjected to the strict discipline of any artistic traditions in the family or elsewhere. Painting, poetry, acting, music were all as close to him as a scholarly education and future; a superficial observer might draw the conclusion that he was born to be a dilettante".—In reality, if you look not just superficially, but with passion and admiration, you can say, at the risk of being misunderstood, that Wagner's art is the product of dilettantism,

albeit one monumentalized by the highest exertions of will-power
and intelligence and raised to the level of genius. The idea of
uniting all the arts is itself dilettantish and, in the absence of the
supreme effort entailed in subjecting them all to his overwhelming
genius for expression, it would have remained at the level of
dilettantism. There is something dubious about his relations with
the arts; insane though it sounds, there is something inartistic
about it.'[1]

Clumsy errors in part writing and in linking chords are in fact
not eliminated until *Lohengrin*; slips in modulation, in harmonic
balance can still be found in *The Mastersingers*. Wagner not only
found it hard to achieve standards of good musicianship – the
archetypal cells of his work are devoid of a primary relationship to
their material. *Leubald* and *The Fairies*, the *Liebesverbot* and *Rienzi*
are all of a piece with those plays of which high-school pupils are
wont to write in their exercise books the title, the Dramatis
Personae and the words 'Act I'.[2] If it is objected that such
beginnings are universal, particularly with dramatists, the answer
must be that Wagner remained faithful all his life to the colossal
format of such works as well as to the costume-fantasies of the
amateur stage; and in the same spirit he actually completed projects
dating back to his earliest years, projects of the sort that normally
do not progress beyond the titles. In his oeuvre, fidelity to a
childhood dream is inseparable from infantility. From the very
first day he was the author of his collected works, and if you read
the detailed diary entries of his reading from the Bayreuth period,
it is difficult to avoid the conclusion that till the end of his days the
entire pleasure of reading was inseparable from the thought of
rows of classics bound in gold. Even his boldest masterstrokes were

---

[1] Thomas Mann '*Leiden und Grösse* Richard Wagners', in *Adel des Geistes*,
Stockholm 1948, p. 402.

[2] *Leubald*, which Wagner completed in 1828, was an example of the adolescent
play to which Adorno is referring. It was a hotchpotch of melodramatic scenes
borrowed from Shakespeare, the young Goethe and Kleist. *The Fairies* (1834) was
Wagner's first completed opera. Subtitled a Romantic Opera, it was avowedly
based on Weber and Marschner. It was not produced in his lifetime. *Translator's
note.*

unable to overcome the fundamental stance of the amateur, that of enthusiastic respect. The path of his development is that of enthusiastic flight from the dilettantism of enthusiasts into the transcendental realm beyond the footlights, much in the same way as he flees the world of victims to which he belongs. He always retained something of the saucy eagerness to learn that is typical of the person who imitates what is already tried and tested. At the same time he assumes the manner of the conductor in command of his orchestra—'Neither king nor emperor—but just to stand there and conduct . . .'[3]—that is one of his decisive childhood experiences. The conductor can do as an expert what the amateur in the auditorium would like to achieve for himself, and by switching on his own excitement he can give objective form to the latter's secondary enthusiasm. He is 'neither king nor emperor', but one of the mass of citizens; yet he enjoys unlimited symbolic power over them. Retreating from the prose of quotidian reality to the point where the backdrop of the stage prevents him from going any further, he does not for a moment break off contact with the non-initiated whom he desires to impress. The dilettantish features in Wagner's character are inseparable from those of his conformism, of his resolute collusion with the public. Enthroned as conductor, he is able to enforce this collusion whilst maintaining the appearance of strongly individual opposition, and to establish the power of impotence in the realm of aesthetics. He not only took up the bourgeois profession of conductor, he was also the first composer to write conductor's music in the grand style. This is not said with the intention of echoing the threadbare reproaches of unoriginality, or with the design of unduly emphasizing mere orchestral skill—something that pales by the side of Wagner's overpowering art of instrumentation. What it alludes to is the fact that his music is conceived in terms of the gesture of striking a blow and that the whole idea of beating is fundamental to it. Through such a system of gestures Wagner's social impulses are translated into technique. If even in his day the composer was already estranged lyrically from the listener, then the tendency of Wagner's music is to disguise that estrangement by incorporating

[3] Hildebrandt, p. 9.

the public in the work as an element of its 'effect'. As advocate of the effect, the conductor is the advocate of the public in the work. As the striker of blows, however, the composer-conductor gives the claims of the public a terrorist emphasis. Democratic considerateness towards the listener is transformed into connivance with the powers of discipline: in the name of the listener, anyone whose feelings accord with any yardstick other than the beat of the music is silenced. From the outset the estrangement from the public is inseparable from the calculation of the effect on the public; only an audience whose social and aesthetic assumptions are so far removed from those of the artist as is the case under high capitalism can become the reified object of calculation by the artist.

Among the functions of the leitmotiv can be found, alongside the aesthetic one, a commodity-function, rather like that of an advertisement: anticipating the universal practice of mass culture later on, the music is designed to be remembered, it is intended for the forgetful. And if the capacity for musical understanding is equated, broadly speaking, with the ability to remember and anticipate, then the old anti-Wagner slur that he was writing for the unmusical can be said to have a certain critical justification, alongside its reactionary message. In the *Symphonie fantastique*, Berlioz's *idée fixe*, the immediate predecessor of the leitmotiv, serves as the sign of an obsession which subsequently reappears at the heart of Baudelaire's work under the title of *spleen*. It is something you cannot get away from. Confronted with its irrational superiority, its seal of unmistakability, the individual subject has no alternative but to capitulate. According to Berlioz's programme, the *idée* appears to a man under the spell of an opium dream. It is the exteriorized projection of something secretly subjective and at the same time ego-alien, to which the ego abandons itself as to a mirage. The Wagnerian leitmotiv remains rooted in these origins. It determines the absence of genuinely constructed motivs in favour of a kind of associative procedure. What psychology a century later was to refer to as ego-weakness is something on which Wagner's music is already predicated.

A similar point is perhaps being made by Steuermann's illuminating comment that, compared to Viennese classicism,

Wagner's music reckons with people who listen to it from a great distance, much as impressionist paintings require to be viewed from a greater distance than earlier painting. To listen from a greater distance also means listening less attentively. The audience of these giant works lasting many hours is thought of as unable to concentrate—something not unconnected with the fatigue of the citizen in his leisure time. And while he allows himself to drift with the current, the music, acting as its own impresario, thunders at him in endless repetitions to hammer its message home. This is possible because it is conceived from the conductor's point of view. As late as the seventeenth century conductors used a heavy stick to beat out the rhythm: both percussion and conducting hark back to their barbaric origins and the idea of a conductorless orchestra is not without its justification. With Wagner however the primacy of the conductor in the composition is unchallenged. Alfred Lorenz, the first person to have tackled the problem of Wagnerian form seriously, unwittingly comes very close to the same discovery: 'May I be permitted at this point to make a personal remark. My understanding of the relationships explained here was facilitated by my own practical experience at the rostrum. For the artist who can free himself from the scholarly study of a score in his home in order to conduct an orchestra, the solution to the problem of the relationship between the form of a work and what it is meant to express, becomes readily apparent. At first artistically, intuitively, through the musical pace of the work itself; and then rationally, as a consequence of the need to achieve complete control over the work by memorizing it.'[4]

If that is so, the key to Wagner's form would lie in the fact that the conductor has to know the work by heart: the analysis of form serves as an aid to memory. Wagner's work, however, actually gives grounds for the supposition that the conductor, in analysing and reproducing the music, traverses the same path as Wagner had done in creating it, but in the opposite direction. The giant packages of his operas are divided up by the notion of striking, of beating time. The whole of the music seems to have been worked

---

[4] Alfred Lorenz, *Das Geheimnis der Form bei Richard Wagner*, Vol. 1, *Der musikalische Aufbau des Bühnenfestspieles Der Ring des Nibelungen*, Berlin 1924, p. 10.

out first in terms of the beat, and then filled in; over great stretches, especially in the early stages of the actual music-drama style, the time seems to be a kind of abstract framework. The whole of *Lohengrin*, with the exception of a tiny part, is written in regular time, as if the evenness of the beat allowed entire scenes to be grasped at a glance, rather like simplifying fraction-sums by 'cancelling'. The transparency of the composition sketch structured in this way inspired Lorenz to make the astonishing remark: 'If you have completely mastered a major work in all its details, you sometimes experience moments in which your consciousness of time suddenly disappears and the entire work seems to be what one might call "spatial", that is, with everything present simultaneously in the mind with precision.'[5] This spatialization suggests that from the composer's vantage point, the Wagnerian forms function as mnemonics. Of course, Lorenz's comment goes far beyond Wagner and would find its true object in Beethoven. In contrast to the symphonic method, Wagner's use of the beat to control time is abstract; it is no more than the idea of time as something articulated by the beat and then projected onto the larger periods. The composer pays no heed to what takes place within time. If the formal division into periods is useful to the performer as a way of dividing up the musical continuum into ordered sections, for the composer the use of the beat is a fallacious method of mastering the empty time with which he begins, since the measure to which he subjects time does not derive from the musical content, but from the reified order of time itself. Hence Lorenz's discovery of the spatialization of time in Wagner is an illusion: the total domination of the beat can only be completely maintained in secondary, uncharacteristic sections, and the many complaints about Wagner's melodic weakness have their foundations not in a straightforward lack of 'ideas', but in the beating gesture that dominates his work.

The marks it leaves on the work are the pretentious pieces of incidental music that punctuate it: flourishes, signals and fanfares. They survive in the midst of the *durchkomponiert* style in which they are deposited like sediment. The conductor conquers the stage

---

[5] Ibid., p. 292.

from the orchestra pit: virtually the whole of *Rienzi* could be played on the stage as a single fanfare. Paul Bekker has drawn attention to the signal-like quality of the themes in the *Dutchman*. [6] It would be possible to trace a crucial stratum of Wagner's practice as a composer back to the tradition of incidental music and its derivatives—such as the orchestra gesture after 'Wolfram von Eschenback, begin. . .'. [7] In fact the Wagner of the middle phase composed an entire form, the introduction to Act III, sc. 3 of *Lohengrin*, simply from fanfares. In all probability this form served as a model for Siegfried's Rhine journey in *The Twilight of the Gods*: even the principle of *fugato*, with its roots in the tradition of absolute music, still bears the marks of its contact with the gesticulating music of the stage. Wherever the abstract beat gains the ascendancy over the musical content, the formulae of incidental music recur; in the later works they form the real counterweight to the chromaticism. With its lack of melodic clarity, its mere gesturing towards harmony, the recitative *parlando* adds to this effect. Interspersed through the highly organized style, one element of unsublimated material remains. His musical consciousness exhibits one peculiar instance of regression: it is as if the aversion to mimicry, which became increasingly powerful with the growth of Western rationalization and which played a by no means insignificant role in crystallizing out the autonomous, quasi-linguistic logic of music, did not have complete power over him. His music lapses into the pre-linguistic, without being able to divest itself wholly of quasi-linguistic elements. Wagnerian 'theatricality', that repellent aspect of his composition which Paul Bekker rightly diagnoses as the innermost kernel of the Wagnerian art-work, is grounded in this regression. Faults of compositional technique in his music always stem from the fact that the musical logic, which is everywhere assumed by the material of his age, is softened up and replaced by a sort of gesticulation, rather in the way that agitators substitute linguistic gestures for the discursive exposition of their thoughts. It is no doubt true that all music has its roots in gesture of this kind and harbours it within itself. In the

[6] Cf. Paul Bekker, *Wagner. Das Leben im Werke*, Berlin, Leipzig 1924, p. 130.
[7] *Tannhäuser*, Act II, sc. 4.

West, however, it has been sublimated and interiorized into ⟨expression,⟩ while at the same time the principle of construction subjects the overall flow of the music to a process of logical synthesis; great music strives for a balance of the two elements. Wagner's position lies athwart this tradition. No historical process is enacted in his music; in this lies his resemblance to the spirit of Schopenhauer's philosophy. The uncontrollably intensified expressive impulse can barely be contained within the interior, within historical consciousness, and finds release as external gesture. It is this that gives the listener the embarrassing feeling that someone is constantly tugging at his sleeve. The strength of the constructivist element is consumed by this exteriorized, quasi-physical intensity. This exteriorization then merges with the fact of reification, of commoditization, just as the late discontent with culture, identical with the discontent of Freudian theory, is responsible for archaizing culture. The element of gesture in Wagner is not, as he claims, the utterance of undivided man, but a reflex that imitates a reified, alienated reality. It is in this manner that the world of gestures is drawn into the artistic effect, into the relationship with the public. Wagnerian gestures were from the outset translations onto the stage of the imagined reactions of the public—the murmurings of the people, applause, the triumph of self-confirmation, or waves of enthusiasm. In the process their archaic muteness, their lack of language, proves its worth as a highly contemporary instrument of domination that fits the public the more exactly, the more high-handedly it confronts it. The conductor–composer both represents and suppresses the bourgeois individual's demand to be heard. He is the spokesman for all and so encourages an attitude of speechless obedience in all. This is why he must strive to breathe life into gestures and to objectify spirit in the shape of gestures. But the two things are incompatible; alienated externality cannot be reconciled with the internality that, in the form of Wagnerian expression, shatters any substantive subjectivity. This is where Wagner's music encounters its innermost contradiction, technical as well as social.

As far as technique is concerned, the motiv is the bearer of that contradiction. Historically, incidental music and the leitmotiv are mediated by the ritornello in the form it had assumed in the older opera down to Weber. Orchestral passages inserted during the recitative have the function of gestures. Like incidental music, they interrupt the singing, and indeed the whole texture of the composition, and mimic the actions of the figures on stage. To that extent they have an intermittent character. However, since they are heard not on the stage but in the orchestra, they also form part of the composition and not just of the action. Mozart and, above all, Weber charged them with expression. It was in this form that Wagner inherited them. In his work the intermittent gesture becomes the fundamental principle of composition. As incidental music and the vehicle of expression at one and the same time, it sheds its interpolatory quality and, as heir to that collective, political reality, to that objectivity of the 'political intrigue' enshrined in the same Grand Opera whose externality Wagner had criticized, it spreads out and pervades the entire work. The device used by Wagner to unite inwardness and objectivity is the sequence. With the aid of the sequence the scheme of abstract symmetrical relationships, with their panoramic architectonics, can be given a firm temporal structure. At the same time, he strives by a process of intensification to reconcile their content with subjective dynamics. The Wagnerian gesture becomes a 'motiv' the moment it is made part of a sequence. Guido Adler has rightly focused his criticism of Wagnerian form on this point. Lorenz's defence remains formalistic because he defines the sequence in static architectonic terms in such a way as to exclude Wagner, whereas in fact the overlay of gesture and expression imports the static principle of the sequence into the functional dynamics of harmony. Wagner's use of the sequence is in the starkest possible contrast to the symphonic sequence of Beethoven. It excludes the analytic instrumentation of Viennese classicism on principle. Gestures can be repeated and intensified but not actually 'developed'. Viennese antiphony had transmuted everything of a gestural nature into intellectual development. Nothing remained to Wagner but to transform this forcibly back into dance or its 'apotheosis', just as in the older suite form from which the sonata form had sprung, the overture was distinguished from the movements which followed it by the fact that it was not itself a stylized dance-form. Sonata and symphony both make time their subject; through the substance they impart to it, they force it to manifest itself. If in the symphony the passage of time is converted into a moment, then by contrast, Wagner's gesture is essentially immutable and atemporal. Impotently repeating itself, music abandons the struggle within the temporal framework it mastered in the symphony.

The reiterated gestures founder amidst the currents from which only a process of transformation could rescue them: the transformation by virtue of which they would cease to be gestures. Thus the attempt to create form by repeating expression-laden gestures is a blind alley. Every repetition of gestures evades the necessity to create musical time; they merely order themselves, as it were, in time and detach themselves from the temporal continuum that they seemingly constituted. It may well be that the uninitiated listener, whose reaction to one of Wagner's mature works is one of boredom, does not simply reveal a pedestrian consciousness incapable of responding to Wagner's claims to the sublime. This failure may instead be caused in part by the flawed nature of the experience of time in the music itself. The difficulty is increased by the fact that the expression that is supposed to lead from one gesture to the next within the sequence—in the most celebrated case, that of the opening of *Tristan*, it is the gesture of 'languishing'—precludes an exact, dance-like repetition, and instead calls for the sort of far-reaching variations that the gestural motivs resist and which are replaced by the Wagnerian principle of 'psychological variation' in a highly artificial manner that does violence to the musical characterization. The repetition of gestures is compulsive, but the repetition of expressions is tautological. The Wagnerian *longueurs*, the garrulousness which goes naturally with the plaintive, cajoling manner of the man, are thus rediscovered in the microcosm of the musical form. Thanks to the repetitions and the dramatization of gesture the expression is falsified. Built into the whole structure and reified, the mimetic impulse degenerates into mere imitation and, ultimately, utter mendacity. So the element of falsehood in Wagner's expression can be traced right down into the origins of his compositional practice. And where the form miscarries, the content too is affected. In the dubious quid pro quo of gestural, expressive and structural elements on which Wagnerian form feeds, what is supposed to emerge is something like an epic totality, a rounded and complete whole of inner and outer. Wagner's music simulates this unity of the internal and external, of subject and object, instead of giving shape to the rupture between them. In this way the process of composition becomes the agent of ideology even before the latter is imported into the music dramas via literature. Nowhere is this more apparent than in those passages where the music glorifies the characters and ascribes to them a noble purity and innocence. The intent to characterize, which converts the musical gesture into the bearer of such expression, inevitably entails an element of reflection and hence always displays purity and innocence as if it were admiring itself in the mirror, thus negating their effect. This is not simply to be explained psychologically, in terms of the dubious 'emotions' of the composer, but must be seen as arising from the fatal logic of the situation. If the expression is to exteriorize itself as sensuous gesture in the way Wagner's practice requires, it is not able to rest content with unassuming self-statement: it is forced to assert itself pointedly and the intensified process of repetition inevitably leads to overstatement. The mere fact of repeating something in an identical form involves an element of reflection. When the impulse to express something occurs a second time, it turns into an underscored commentary on itself. Conversely, by decking out the external elements derived from incidental music with the trappings of subjectivity, Wagner achieves only that cloud of hot air that Nietzsche mistrusted as much as the purity. The latter is dissipated amidst all the ostentation, while for its part the carnival is sacrificed to the solemn stage festival [*Bühnen-weihfestspiel*].

Wagner's strength, however, proves itself in his efforts to master the contradiction, which to a man with his technical expertise must have revealed itself at every step. If there is a 'mystery of form' in his case, then it must be sought in that desperate, never acknowledged and wholly muted struggle. Lorenz discerns the clue to such a mystery in the principle of the 'Bar' stanza, the strophic form of *Minnesang* and *Meistergesang*, with its *a-a-b* scheme consisting of two equal *pedes* and a *cauda* diverging from them.[8] This archaic schema dominates *The Mastersingers* and the aesthetic debates within it. But Wagner's use of this stanza is by no means restricted to limited, relatively autonomous passages like the Prize Song. Lorenz is able to trace its influence through the larger structures and in his discussion of the parallels between the first two acts gets so carried away as to conclude that the entire opera is nothing but one gigantic 'Bar' stanza.[9]

The same feature can be discerned also in the elements of the individual motivs. It is here that the gestural nature of the 'Bar'-form becomes apparent. Its origins can be seen clearly in the earlier works. Think of the start of Act II, scene 2 of *Tannhäuser*, directly following Elisabeth's aria. There, after a prolonged introductory chord, an eight-bar stanza occurs. The first *Stollen* is a shy, tentative two-bar motiv. Slightly varied, and extended by half a bar, it appears as the second *Stollen*, transposed upwards. This is rather like what happens later on with the first sequence of Wagner's typical motivs which on the whole, however, seldom permit such variations in his mature style and, particularly in *Tristan*, rest content with the transposition upwards. The *Abgesang*, which is again half a bar longer, is supplied by a 'very lively' semiquaver-figure that soars high above the rise of the motiv but then swiftly collapses when the wind instruments break off. The dramatic meaning of the passage is that Tannhäuser, shyly, hesitantly, and unnoticed, approaches his beloved, and then, encouraged by Wolfram, throws himself 'impetuously at Elizabeth's feet', remaining there until she bids him rise. It is the third gesture, the *Abgesang*, that is decisive here. It strikes out boldly and then returns to its starting-point, just as the singer lets his outstretched arms drop when he reaches Elizabeth and clings to her without moving,

---

[8] The strophe of *Minnesang* and *Meistergesang*, known as a *Bar*, consists of two sections, an *Aufgesang* which is itself divided into two equal parts called *Stollen* or *pedes*, and an *Abgesang* or *cauda*. The basic structure is found in the division of the sonnet into $4+4+6$ lines. More simply, it can be seen in Good King Wenceslas where the *Abgesang* repeats the *Aufgesang* metrically, but differs from it in melody. *Translator's note.*

[9] Lorenz, Vol. 3, *Der musikalische Aufbau von Richard Wagners 'Die Meister-singer von Nürnberg'*, Berlin 1931, p. 10.

silently turned in on himself. A pause follows the sustained second inversion of the dominant seventh; it is a model of that strange pause that constantly determines Wagner's music despite all its dynamism and in fact in the very midst of it. The expansive gesture recoils back to the body. Its collapse is like the collapse of a wave. This is perhaps why Wagner's musical gestures are reminiscent of dance-movements, and why the repetition of the motivs usurps the symmetry of the dance—because it is only as dancers that men can imitate the waves. Wagner's use of the wave as a form is his attempt at a musical resolution to the contradiction between expression and gesture, long before he rationalized it in terms of Schopenhauer's philosophy. His aim is to reconcile the lack of development in the gesture with the unrepeatable finality of the expression by making the gesture countermand itself. Itself and also time. If Wagner does not dominate time like Beethoven, neither does he fulfil it like Schubert. He revokes it. The eternity of Wagnerian music, like that of the poem of the *Ring*, is one which proclaims that nothing has happened; it is a state of immutability that refutes all history by confronting it with the silence of nature. The Rhine maidens who are playing with the gold at the start of the opera and receive it back at the end are the final statement both of Wagner's wisdom and of his music. Nothing is changed; and it is the dynamics of the individual parts that reinstate the amorphous primal condition. The forces that are unleashed end up sustaining the state of immutability and hence the powers that be—the very powers they had set out to overthrow. This is more clearly inscribed in the formal principles underlying his music than it ever was in his philosophical opinions. Contrary to Schopenhauer, however, is the creation of a comforting equilibrium, the aesthetic consecration of everything that is insufferable in the actual social reality from which his work is attempting to flee.

The Mastersingers provides astounding evidence of the ideo-logical nature of 'the mystery of form'. The songs sung by the members of the educated classes, by those antipodes. Walther and Beckmesser, cling to the 'Bar'-form. However, Sachs, who exercises a right to protest which he derives from 'the people', and who makes the ambiguous claim that 'I've mainly written street songs',[10] sings a straightforward strophic song. Thus *The Master-singers*, the greatest testimony to Wagner's self-awareness, ac-credits the 'Bar'-form to the notables and to the ruling class. If, however, we accept Lorenz's analysis and so characterize the entire oeuvre in terms of the 'Bar'-stanza, then within the economy of *The Mastersingers* as a whole, the upper class is as much in the right as are the Rhine maidens in the *Ring*. For in that work they, the allegories of that sea to which the Wagnerian dream regresses, are similarly vindicated at the expense of Alberich, the parvenu.

This insight into the function of the 'Bar'-form implies a critique of Wagner's form in general. Lorenz, who pointedly took issue with the reactionary cliché about Wagner's lack of form that had been parroted ever since Nietzsche, was more interested in the organization of the large-scale forms than in the 'themes'. He justified this with the claim that the analysis of motivs had been adequately carried out by Wolzogen and other so-called works of practical guidance. But it was a mistake to have allowed himself to confuse a musical analysis of motivs—which would derive the large-scale form from the way in which the thematic cells are developed and varied—with the kind of poeticizing catalogue of leitmotivs that discovers a musical parallel for every line in the text. The real justification for his lack of interest in detail lies in the nature of Wagner's work itself. In the relevant chapter of Volume I of his book, Lorenz says: 'The main feature that catches our attention is that this arrangement'—Wagner's exposition of his themes—'regularly takes the form of frequent repetition so that the motiv is clearly imprinted on our minds.'[11] It is the repetition of the motivs, whether in identical or systematically transposed and graduated form, that absolves Lorenz from the need to provide analyses of the type exemplified by Berg's discussion of Schoenberg. But this abstinence implies that, at the level of detail, there is really nothing to analyse in Wagner's music. Wagner knows about motivs and large-scale forms—but not about themes. Repetition poses as development, transposition as thematic work, and, conversely, the lyrical song, essentially unrepeatable, is treated

[10] Act II, sc. 6.
[11] Lorenz, Vol. I, p. 75.

as if it were a dance. The use of the 'Bar'-form to reverse his ostensible meaning has the effect of simply dissolving all un-resolved contradictions into thin air. Whereas Wagner's music incessantly arouses the appearance, the expectation and the demand for novelty, strictly speaking nothing new takes place in it.

This discovery is the grain of truth contained in the charge of formlessness. But the formlessness is the product not of chaos, but of a false identity. Identical materials put in an appearance as if they were something new and thereby substitute the abstract succession of bars for the dialectical progression of substance, its inner historicity. Wagner's form is an empty shell: the unfolding in time to which it lays claim is inauthentic. The large-scale forms discovered by Lorenz are superimposed from outside and end up as the nameless schematic patterns that they are when they articulate the abstract beat at the outset. It is no accident that Lorenz's analyses can be tabulated, for in principle a table is as inimical to the passage of time as Wagnerian form itself. For all their meticulous-ness they are nothing more than a graphic game, without power over the actual music. Wagner's forms, even the paradoxical 'Bar'-form which negates the flow of time within which it moves, all fail to do justice to time. Mephistopheles's saying, 'It might just as well never have been', has the final word. Hence the disillusionment, the disappointed expectations—and this from a man who in private life was as ready as the artist in his work to break his promises. His music acts as if time had no end, but its effect is merely to negate the hours it fills by leading them back to their starting-point.

3
Motiv

The inexorable progression that fails to create any new quality and constantly flows into the already known, the ⟨dynamics of permanent regression,⟩ have endowed Wagner's work with an enigmatic quality and even today, in contrast with almost all other music, the listener is left with the sense of a blind spot, of something unresolved—notwithstanding his familiarity with the music. Wagner denies the listener who accompanies him the satisfaction of a thing clearly defined and it is left in doubt whether the formal meaning of a given moment has been rightly apprehended. Sachs's words—'I can't hold on to it—but nor can I forget it'[1]—are an allusion to this. Nothing is unambiguous. What was once felt to be irritatingly modern about him and what critics described, somewhat unmusically, as nervousness and hyper-sensitivity, is rooted in this ambiguity of musical meaning. Of course, there is also an ideological ambiguity to match it, ranging from his well-known ambivalence between sexuality and asceticism to the role of ambiguous figures such as Hagen, who is both 'warrior' and traitor, Kundry, who is both penitent and seductress, and even heroes like Tristan and Siegfried, the faithless faithful. Ambiguity is no stranger to the Romantic tradition of composition: the equivocal altered chords of Schubert are of this kind, and Wagner, whose work might seem to have little in common with Schubert's, uses such chords for preference. But he is the first in whom ambiguity has been elevated to a principle of style and for whom the category of the 'interesting', as opposed to the logicality

---

[1] *The Mastersingers*, Act I, sc. 3.

of musical language, has become dominant. It is this that excited Baudelaire, the most advanced musical consciousness of his day, even though he obviously did not even know *Tristan*—to say nothing of its effect upon Nietzsche. What is new here is not the musical identity that is preserved amid all the changes. That had already been perfected by Viennese Classicism, and above all by Beethoven, who constructed the most total musical unity in multiplicity. But it was achieved in accordance with the logic of the firmly established musical language appropriate to a society that still cohered despite all the antagonisms within it. Ever since the explosion of individuality in Berlioz, composers had been eager to express the sentiments of their adventitious uniqueness. Accordingly, they dismissed this logic as irrational and opposed to it the principle of surprise. Such sentiments had been alien to Classicism, or at least domesticated by formal synthesis. Wagner's art lacks the strength to do likewise: the weaker the social and hence, too, the aesthetic determination of the ego became, and the less it was able to exteriorize itself as an objective expression of a totality, the greater the arrogance with which an unfettered individuality asserted itself. By reflecting and displaying its own weakness, the ego differentiates itself infinitely, but by the same token that weakness causes it to regress to a pre-ego stage. Hence, in the predominance of the psychological and of the ambiguously interesting in Wagner, an historical moment becomes visible. But the fault-line discernible in Wagner's work—his impotence in the face of the technical contradictions and the social conflicts underlying them, in short all the qualities that prompted his contemporaries to speak of 'decadence'—is also the path of artistic progress.

Paul Bekker regarded expression as Wagner's basic category. But nowhere does the hidden flaw, the abyss lying beneath the densely textured surface of his integrated compositional style, become more apparent than here. If the synthesis of gesture and expression in the leitmotiv does not come off, if the motiv, as the bearer of expression, insists at the same time on its character as gesture, then the gesture is never able to express an emotional content directly. Instead it presents us with that content. What specifically characterizes Wagnerian expression is its intention-

ality: the motiv is a sign that transmits a particle of congealed
meaning. For all its intensity and emphasis, Wagner's music is as
script is to words and it is hard to avoid the suspicion that its
intensity is needed only to conceal that fact. Its expression does not
present itself, but is itself the object of presentation. Wagner's
leitmotivs stand revealed as allegories that come into being when
something purely external, something that has fallen out of the
framework of a spiritual totality, is appropriated by meanings and
made to represent them, a process in which signifiers and signified
are interchangeable. The allegorical arts of *The Mastersingers*, for
example, the ubiquitous artificial use of allegorical names and,
finally, the entire abstract structure of meanings behind the *Ring*,
are no mere epiphenomena: it is precisely such seeming eccentri-
cities that actually give the game away. The leitmotiv has a history
that goes back via Berlioz to the programme music of the
seventeenth century, when a generally binding musical logic did
not yet exist, and its origins here only begin to make sense in the
context of allegory, rather than the childish games with echo-
effects and the like. Dear though the hackneyed concept of the
symbol is to orthodox Wagnerian scholars, they have nevertheless
drawn attention inadvertently to the allegorical character of the
leitmotivs by giving each one a definite name, rather like the
inscriptions that provide the key to the allegorical pictures to
which they are attached. If there is no movement at the macro-
level of Wagner's music, because it rescinds its own temporal flow,
it is no less true that the details too are marked by a rigid stasis. The
leitmotivs are miniature pictures, and their supposed psychological
variations involve only a change of lighting. They remain more
loyal than they imagine to Berlioz's term, the *idée fixe*, and it is
their inflexibility that sets limits to and even negates the psychological dynamism. In *The Twilight of the Gods*, where a dynamic
style of composition is applied to an older set of motivs of the
greatest allegorical brittleness, the contradiction is quite obvious.
Whereas the purpose of the leitmotiv is to serve the metaphysical
ends of the music dramas, as the finite sign of allegedly infinite
ideas, in reality it becomes their enemy: in the womb of Wagner's
late-Romanticism, a positivistic element is engendered, not unlike
the positivist and scientific twist given to Kantian idealism by

Schopenhauer's metaphysics. Even in Wagner's own day the public made a crude link between the leitmotivs and the persons they characterized and this was possible because they had not completely merged with the mental significations with which they claimed to be identical: from the outset the necessity for commentaries revealed the bankruptcy of Wagner's own aesthetics of immediate unity. The degeneration of the leitmotiv is implicit in this: via the ingenious illustrative technique of Richard Strauss it leads directly to cinema music where the sole function of the leitmotiv is to announce heroes or situations so as to help the audience to orientate itself more easily.

Allegorical rigidity has infected the motiv like a disease. The gesture becomes frozen as a picture of what it expresses. But by the same token it calls a halt to the sheer flow and gives birth to resistances of construction. Only in an articulated harmonic framework is it possible for the motiv to take its place and for the technique of the developing sequence to generate that allegorical meaning which the leitmotiv requires and which is formalized to a great extent in the three-part 'Bar'-form. This can be illustrated even in the case of what seem to be purely chromatic models, such as the much analysed opening of *Tristan*. The need for a mode of articulation that would enable the formal meaning to unfold gradually generates a strengthened tonality as a counter-tendency to the chromatic harmony, and variation as a counter-balance to the ordinary sequence. In the first repetition of the opening motiv the major sixth supplants the minor sixth of the model: B–G $\#$ for A–F. This deviation results from the dependence of the whole sentence on its implied basic key, the harmonic A minor scale, in which we have F *natural*, but G *sharp*. It is transcribed by the selection of the characteristic inflections. The point of paraphrasing within a key while still in the course of chromatic modulation is to unify the latter harmonically and hence to organize it. This however leads in the sequencing process to structural consequences: by means of the harmonic identity the mechanical identity of the two parts of the melodic sequence is avoided. There is a decisive interval separating the model and the first consequent from each other: they are related like a theme to its rudimentary variation. Without variation, the sequence group would lead to

the dominant seventh of B, whereas when varied it leads to that of
C major as the relative major key of A minor. In this way the
relation to the basic key is strengthened. Precisely by holding fast
to the unity of the key of A minor, and so resisting the unrestrained
levelling process of continual modulation, the banality of the
chromatic sequence is eliminated and that autonomy of chromatically adjacent notes is anticipated which in Schoenberg became so
much more of a threat to tonality than a simple chromaticism. If
we may venture to compare the 'Bar'-form with the triadic
scheme of the dialectic, then the third member of the sequence, the
Abgesang, would correspond to the synthesis. In order to continue
to guarantee tonal unity it starts not a second but a minor third
higher than the first sequence: yet again a critical interval is varied.
At the same time, as the residue of the second consequent, the start
of the *Abgesang* retains the interval of the major sixth D–B, but by
inserting a second descending second, it restores the original
melodic relation to the initial note in the spirit of the model. As a
negation of the negation, as the retraction of the deviation in the
second phrase of the sequence, the third part affirms the unity of
the whole and gives it a harmonic interpretation by means of the
cadence on the dominant of the dominant of A minor. In the
following *forte* entry the music is actually brought back to A minor
when Wagner now underpins the residue of the motiv, E♯ to
F♯, with the dominant, admittedly once again avoiding the
tonic, by means of the interrupted cadence to the submediant: a
textbook example of what Schoenberg was later to call 'circum-
scribed tonality'. When Lorenz in his criticism of Kurth puts the
emphasis on the diatonic and tectonic aspects of Wagner's music, as
a counter-weight to expressive chromatic features, this is not to be
taken in the sense of some ominously Teutonic state of primal
health that had only once permitted itself the excesses of *Tristan*. It
is rather that, at his greatest moments, Wagner draws his
productive force from an irreducible contradiction, and wrests a
progressive constructiveness from the regressive moment of
gesture. This goes as far beyond mere subjective expression as it
cancels and preserves it in the double Hegelian sense.

What this makes clear, however, is that progress and reaction in
Wagner's music cannot be separated out like sheep and goats. The

two are indissolubly intertwined. Beneath the thin veil of continuous progress Wagner has fragmented the composition into allegorical leitmotivs juxtaposed like discrete objects. These resist the claims both of a totalizing musical form and of the aesthetic claims of 'symbolism', in short, the entire tradition of German idealism. Even though Wagner's music is thoroughly perfected as style, this style is not a system in the sense of being a logically consistent totality, an immanent ordering of parts and whole. But this very fact is not without its revolutionary implications. In art, as in philosophy, the various systems strive to create a synthesis out of diversity. In the process they always let themselves be guided by an existing, but now questionable, totality whose immediate right to exist they dispute even while they indirectly reproduce it. And that is as far as Wagner gets. The reverse side of his apologetic, backward-looking relationship to the bourgeoisie is that he is no longer able to accept the cosmos of bourgeois forms whole-heartedly. Nothing already existing is tolerated, no 'standard forms'—from his large-scale structures which scorn the name of 'opera', down to the arrangement of the motivs which idio-syncratically recoil from anything reminiscent of convention. Nowadays, compared with Wagnerian *décadence*, the ground is being prepared for a new decay inasmuch as musicians have lost their sensitivity in this respect and actually thirst for the fetters of convention which Wagner strove to discard. Few things illumi-nate his attitude better than his remark that, when listening to Mozart, he sometimes imagined he could hear the clatter of the dishes accompanying the music. Contemporary attitudes towards the musical inheritance suffer from the fact that no one has the confidence to be so disrespectful. With its hostility to standard forms and its playful use of them, Wagner's musical form not only does away with the feudal remnants of musical material, it also makes the material incomparably more pliant to the composer's will than ever before. The maxim underlying this approach to form is formulated in lapidary fashion in the aesthetic conversation in *The Mastersingers*: 'How should I start according to the rules?—You frame them yourself and then comply with them.' Wagner's call for a style of declamation that does justice to the text is part of the same phenomenon. It is anti-Romantic and anti-feudal: the idea of musical prose is adumbrated here with the breaking of the magic charm of symmetry. The affinity with language, to which music owes so much of its claim to metaphysical status, is suddenly turned upside down so that it becomes a means of musical enlightenment, admittedly one held in check in Wagner's use of it by the dominance of the symmetrical period. The call for 'natural' declamation is as symptomatic of Wagner's hostility to the standard musical forms as of the need to synthesize the arts; but as in the case of the leitmotiv this too prepares the ground for the technical, rational work of art.

The relationship of the latter to the technique of the leitmotiv is nowhere clearer than in the atomization of the material, which breaks it down into the smallest possible components with the aim of bringing about its subsequent integration in obedience to Siegfried's programme:

> Now I've made shreds of your shining sharpness,
> in the crucible I cook the splinters.

This programme was fully implemented in *Tristan*. It is difficult to avoid the parallel with the quantification of the industrial labour process, its fragmentation into the smallest possible units, just as it is no accident that an act of material production was selected as the allegory of that principle. Broken down into the smallest units, the totality is supposed to become controllable, and it must submit to the will of the subject who has liberated himself from all pre-existing forms. The fact that Wagner should have developed this analogue to the methods of the impressionist painters without at all being aware of it is as potent a testimony of the unity of the productive forces of the age as it is of the screening-off of the individual realms from each other. And if Wagner failed to take the potential impressionism of his technique of the motiv to its logical conclusion—or did so only episodically in mood music— this is as much the result of his attitude towards his public as of his aesthetic principles. From a social point of view, the interlocking of old and new implies that while fresh stimuli are constantly being offered, well-worn habits of listening are never to be affronted. The Wagnerian atmosphere is already smouldering with something of the furious rancour of the Philistine, which later on leads to the anathematization of all 'Isms'. The greater the progress in the technicization of the work of art, the rational planning of its methods and hence of its effects, the more anxiously is Wagner intent upon making his music appear spontaneous, immediate and natural and upon concealing the controlling will. In contradiction to his practice, his ideology denies all dissolving, analytical procedures. We are reminded of the brutal and primitive terms in which Cosima had expressed her summary dismissal of all modern music in her correspondence with the Nazi Chamberlain. Wagner was an impressionist *malgré lui*, as is only to be expected in view of the backward state of the technical and human forces of production and hence too of aesthetic doctrine in Germany in the middle of the nineteenth century. What played a role here, over and above the traditional superstition that the greatness of the aesthetic idea is reflected in the magnitude of the chosen object and the monumentality of the work of art, was a pre-critical view of melody and one inappropriate to Wagner's own position. No comparison of Wagner with the Impressionists will be adequate unless it is remembered that the credo of universal symbolism to which all his technical achievements subscribe is that of Puvis de Chavannes and not Monet's. In Wagner's case what predominates is already the totalitarian and seigneurial aspect of atomization; that devaluation of the individual vis-à-vis the totality, which excludes all authentic dialectical interaction. However, it is not just the nullity of the individual that has such dire implications for the Wagnerian totality, but rather that the atom, the descriptive motiv, must always put in an appearance for the sake of characterization, as if it were something, a claim it cannot always satisfy. In this way the themes and motivs join forces in a sort of pseudo-history. In Wagner's music we can catch a glimpse of that tendency of the late-bourgeois consciousness under the compulsion of which the individual insists the more emphatically on his own importance, the more specious and impotent he has become in reality. Some of the falseness of all this is perceptible in many of the Wagnerian motivs whose rhetorical gesturing overtaxes their real substance, whereas sometimes, of course, they work miraculously well. Once again the formal category as such, the nullity of the motiv as a mere postulate, the ephemeral nature of individuation, is common ground between Wagner and Viennese Classicism. But the meaning of the procedure has been inverted and, therewith, its aesthetic justification. In Beethoven, the isolated occurrence, the 'creative idea' [*Einfall*]², is artistically trivial wherever the idea of totality takes precedence; the motiv is introduced as something quite abstract in itself, simply as the principle of pure becoming, and as the totality emerges from it, the isolated motiv, which is submerged in the whole, is concretized and confirmed by it. In Wagner the over-inflated creative idea denies the triviality that inheres in it by virtue of its status as a prelinguistic gesture. The penalty it must pay for this is that it is itself denied by the development that it proves unable to generate, even though it unceasingly claims to sustain that development and provide it with a model. The seemingly unified totality, which owes its existence to the extirpation of the qualitatively individual, turns out to be mere illusion, a contradiction raised to the level of the absolute.

The more triumphantly Wagner's music resounds, the less capable it is of discovering an enemy to subdue within itself; the triumphant cries of bourgeois victory always drowned out its mendacious claims to have done heroic deeds. It is precisely the absence of any dialectical material on which it could prove itself

---

² Adorno has glossed the concept of *Einfall* in *The Philosophy of Modern Music*, translated by Anne Mitchell and Wesley Bloomster, London 1973, p. 74. 'The concept of *Einfall* was defined in order to distinguish the theme as a matter of organic essence from its creative transformation in the work as a matter of abstract, hypothetical ordering. *Einfall* is not just a psychological category, a matter of "inspiration", but a moment in the dialectical process manifest in musical form. This moment marks the irreducibly subjective element in this process and, by means of its inexplicability, further designates this aspect of music as its essence, while the "working out" represents the process of objectivity and the process of becoming, which to be sure, contains this subjective moment as a driving force. On the other hand, as essence, *Einfall* is also possessed of objectivity. Since Romanticism music has been based upon the conflict and synthesis of these moments. It appears, however, that they resist unification just as strongly as the bourgeois concept of the individual stands in perennial contrast to the totality of the social process. The inconsistency between the theme and what happens to it reflects such social irreconcilability. Nevertheless, composition must keep a firm grasp on the *Einfall* if the subjective moment is not to be lost.' *Einfall* has been translated here as the 'creative idea'. *Translator's note.*

that condemns the Wagnerian totality to mere duration. It is evident that motivs like that of the sword or Siegfried's horn cannot be mastered by any artistic form: the criticism that he has no melodic inventiveness refers less to a failing of the subjective imagination than to an objective lack. The gestural method is repeatedly forced to resort to the melodic sequence of natural overtones. But it is these that demonstrate the limits of the subjective animating power that lays claim to supreme rule. Thus the constant concern for vividness and effect that induces Wagner to employ signal-like motivs actually leads to a lack of vividness and to technical inconsistency. This can be demonstrated as early as the overture to *Lohengrin*. Following four introductory bars, its theme is expounded in an eight-bar phrase. The first half feels unarticulated: the poetic idea of 'hovering' seems, as it were, to prevent a logical musical development, whereas, technically, the aesthetic idea of vagueness actually stands in need of precise definition. The paucity of articulation in this first half does not just derive from its relation to the second whose formal meaning— whether as melodic continuation or as consequent—does not emerge with clarity. Even the melody of the antecedent somehow slips from one's grasp because it becomes obsessed with the two notes E and F♯ without their repetition's being made unambiguously thematic. The reason for this is in the first instance harmonic. Apart from the tonic and dominant, the antecedent makes use only of the submediant, which in the context of the phrase remains dependent, a mere substitute for the tonic. The indecisive harmonic relations between the first and the sixth scale degree are reflected in the lack of melodic articulation of the interval E natural–F♯, the notes into which the top voice always lapses, as it were. The small variety of the chords is itself the product of the economy of the passage. The secondary triads (some of which are tonicized by local modulation), or put simply, the fresh notes of the lower voice, are saved up for the consequent which has to make do with the same material as the antecedent. In the consequent, then, the melody, even though it remains fixated on the same notes as the antecedent, E and F♯ minor, suddenly gains in plasticity, thanks to the harmonic perspective opened up by the contact with the keys of F♯ minor, E major and B minor.

But Wagner can make only sparing use of the harmonic perspective to produce this melodic plasticity, not merely because he always has to reckon with excessively long intervals of time, but also because he has one eye on the requirements of the conductor and the overall effect. Paradoxically, both in theory and in his own practice, Wagner's chromaticism never quite loses a certain reserve towards modulation, apart from *Tristan*. Without the counterweight provided by diatonic passages like that of the antecedent, the variety of chords and the chromatic part-writing would lead to that esotericism which Wagner feared like the plague. To pour scorn precisely on that was not the least of the polemical intentions of *The Mastersingers*, where the over-sophisticated *Meistergesang* is contrasted with the unrestrained healthy instincts of the people: the idea of retracting his own innermost beliefs reaches right into the history of Wagner's own work, which stands in something of the same relation to its productive centre, *Tristan*, as the Rider over Lake Constance.[3]

The socially conformist requirement of comprehensibility and the aesthetic requirement of vividness—which originally coincided in Wagner—now diverge. The antinomy they contain, the demand that everything should be both comprehensible and distinctive, affects both aspects of his work equally, both the diatonic and the chromatic motivs. The 'distinctive', fascinating semitone-steps of *Tristan* can no more be properly differentiated from each other than, conversely, the would-be primeval fanfares can be retained as melody; particularly since the latter tend towards the amorphous, something that can be seen in fully developed form in the prelude to *Rhinegold*. The rupture extends right to the centre of each creative idea. As a musical category, the creative idea [*Einfall*] is of recent origin. It was as unfamiliar to the seventeenth and early eighteenth centuries as were the property rights to particular melodies. Creative ideas can exist only as the traces that the monadically isolated composer strives to inscribe in the musical material as distinct characters. Wagner's work, however, is intent on causing these inscribed characters to lose their identity and

---

[3] In the poem by Gustav Schwab the traveller rides over Lake Constance, which is completely frozen, unaware of the great risk he is running. It has become proverbial for an innocent venturer. *Translator's note*.

merge in the natural material. The power of protest, which comes to the same thing as the creative idea, is cancelled out in his work, and the more the composer learns how to dominate the alienated musical material, the more it eludes him, until finally, as a desperate resource, he exalts it with the title of essence. The tendency of Wagner's compositional technique as well as that of his texts is to dissolve everything definite and specific into an undifferentiated mass, whether into the 'Ur-triad' or into chromaticism. Wagner's hostility to standard forms ends in absurdity, in the nameless, the unspecific and the abstract—to such an extent that in Max Reger, for example, there is no theme or bar in any work that could not be transposed into any other, while the internal dislocations in the motiv material of his Neo-German successors, Strauss and Pfitzner, became apparent by the extremes of boastful banality and helpless incoherence that characterize them.

These dislocations at the level of detail are reflected in the macrocosm in what was known to the Bayreuth school as unending melody. Even less than elsewhere does this refer to something new: the bombastic term here covers up a weakness. Unending melody as the red thread, the firmly-established line of the main voice, is another feature already found in Viennese Classicism. There the leaping of the melody from one timbre to another had made the unity of the orchestration more tangible. With his mind on the 'elevated style' that inspired his entire work and which he opposed to the secluded happiness of petty-bourgeois music, Wagner was unique in protesting against music set apart in particular genres, music that could be easily summed up. He still found Brahms irritating in this respect and hence his allusion, in the course of his quarrel with Nietzsche, to 'the ditty of Triumph or Destiny' [*Triumph- oder Schicksalsliedchen*]. Outwardly the melodic flow is kept as continuous as possible and since the listener's memory is denied any small-scale musical unit to latch on to, this has the effect of harnessing him all the more inexorably within the total effect. The unending melody progressively gains the upper hand over those discretely contrasting, inadequately connected periods, the preferred form of a Romanticism that had surrendered to the intimate so completely as to be ready and willing to reduce the sonata to conformity with the ideal of the *Lied*. Partly by inclination, partly from necessity, the melody of his German predecessors had become increasingly limited in scope—to say nothing of the use of melody in favourite operas of the first part of the nineteenth century. And when this is contrasted with Wagner's use of large-scale melodic complexes, the latter can be seen to signify progress in a similar sense, and a similarly suspect sense at that, to that in which the industrial upsurge of the Bismarckian era is progress when measured against the world of the pre-1848 period.

In the most successful passages of *The Mastersingers*, in Act III of *Siegfried* and on occasion in *The Valkyrie*, Wagner does in fact achieve a hitherto unprecedented melodic flexibility: as if the melodic impulse had liberated itself from the fetters of the small-scale period, as if the force of urgency and expression surged far beyond the bounds of conventional structures and symmetrical proportions. But as a complement to the technique of the motiv, the unending melody, too, remains an illusion. Not that it lacked articulation; the fact that Nietzsche found Wagner formless shows that even he still heard him with the ears of the Biedermeier listener. Initially, however, Wagner's anxiety lest the 'red thread' that had come down from Beethoven might break leads to a loss of differentiation in the melodic flow. Despite everything, in both Wagner and his Romantic predecessors, melody remains far more closely confined to the easily graspable foreground and the top voice than was the case with the Viennese Classical style that had been schooled in the discipline of chamber music. The much-remarked distribution of the melody among the instruments refines it colouristically, rather than making it dialectic in itself, resolving the tensions by means of a genuinely analytic instrumentation. Such a primitive approach is intensified by the rhythmic effects that Wagner himself resisted with a good deal of critical insight in the years separating *Lohengrin* from *Rhinegold*. It arises from the notion of 'infinity', the over-extension of the time-dimension. Many bars are needed to make up a metrical unit and in Wagner's music, as in the *Venusberg*, seven years are just one day. It is only in the larger structures that we find variety. The detail, designed from the outset with an eye on the whole, and without any intrinsic power, drifts into monotony again and again for that very reason. This is particularly marked in *Lohengrin*. Frequently, as in the inspired second act of *Tristan*, the quasi-symphonic movements are constructed by the simple aggregation of lengthy sections, each one of which is powered by a principal motiv until it is exhausted. When the next motiv is finally introduced, the effect is rather of a complete change than of a logical conclusion, and in themselves the sections are astonishingly poor in invention when compared to even the simplest piece by Mozart. This impatience in the main voices, which makes them aspire to attain the dimensions of a large-scale period without any disturbing complications, has the further consequence that all true polyphony is frustrated, despite all the assertions of the Neo-German composers to the contrary. The only strict contrapuntal passages consist of a combination of themes. As in the most celebrated example, the overture to *The Mastersingers*, the highly literary effect of these passages derives from the paradoxical simultaneity of melodies that had originally been conceived of in succession and which are felt to stand in need of a chord accompaniment. They serve only to confirm the fundamental homophony by creating a synthetic apotheosis of the different motivs. Likewise, the much-acclaimed autonomy of the orchestral inner voices, which even served as a model for the early Schoenberg, was harmonically determined, at least in Wagner himself. The inner voices bring about the movement of the chords into each other, and paraphrase them, in accordance with the basic rule that in a four-part harmonic movement the development should proceed in small steps, if possible without any leaps. Over and above this, the autonomiz-ation of the inner voices also satisfies the need for expressiveness. The aim of the composer, with his practical experience of the orchestra, is that as far as possible they should be 'meaningful' to the extent that they can be played with the expression which accumulates to create the effect of the whole. It is undeniable that Wagner's harmonic polyphony contributed decisively to the emergence of independent polyphony. In *Tristan*, *The Twilight of the Gods* and *Parsifal* we can sometimes feel how the secure, four-part harmonic scheme so punctiliously observed by Wagner trembles under the impact of the polyphonic counterpressure. The unending melody itself, however, dependent as it is on the progression of the chords and hardly ever autonomous, derives little benefit from all this. The compulsive renunciation of whole areas of compositional device, which is the inevitable complement of the ruthless imposition of one's own 'style', forces Wagner into those repetitions, spun-out continuations and over-extensions that are all ultimately sustained by a body of motivs that was itself designed exclusively with a view to such infinity. This, and not the emancipation of melody from definite, observable caesuras, must bear the responsibility for those incongruities that Wagner's early listeners had interpreted as proof of his formlessness. Wagner's melody is in fact unable to make good its promise of infinity since, instead of unfolding in a genuinely free and unconstrained manner, it has recourse to small-scale models and by stringing those together provides a substitute for true development. The melodic endings within the unending melody are all too apparent. They are only just negotiated by stereotyped interrupted cadences, such as the 'resolution' of the dominant seventh onto the second inversion of the dominant seventh of the dominant. The pretended infinity remains bad; it is no more than the husk of something finite and the unending melody dares to keep on going only because it feels perfectly secure within the sequence of each section, because ultimately it knows itself to be unchanging.

Hence it is logical that the conception of unending melody should have failed to have any lasting effect. All the more powerful, however, was the impact of a closely related device: the recitative *parlando*. This rests on the premiss that the traditional articulation of the melody is no longer recognized, that horizontal progression is released from the rules governing verses and strophes and that this dispensation is carried over to include the musical treatment of the text itself. This brings us face to face with a social fact. As is well known, the Wagnerian *parlando* is generally considered to have its roots in *recitativo accompagnato*, even though, from the outset, Wagner was at pains to protest against any confusion with recitative. In *Das Liebesverbot* there are occasional examples of the custom borrowed from the *Spieloper* of giving the principal melodic part to the orchestra while the singing voice 'declaims' in accompaniment, for example, by holding on to a note. One might hazard the guess that opera composers such as Rossini and Auber even owe their reputation for wit to idiosyncrasies of this sort. What was probably intended by this was that the *Spieloper*, without sacrificing its purely musical texture, was able by this means to allow the meaning of the words to filter through and so to relax something of the stylistic rigour of grand opera for the benefit of empirical existence. No doubt Wagner borrowed the declamatory use of the singing voice from the genre which he otherwise condemned for its coldness and superficiality. He evidently strove to synthesize the opera buffa and opera seria, just as Viennese Classicism had blended the 'galant' and the 'learned' High Baroque styles. This would mean that the substance of the motivs was derived from the stirring Romantic opera, the relationship between language, song and órchestra from the *Spieloper* and the style of the music drama was based on a union of a diversity of operatic types as had already been attempted in *The Magic Flute*, *Don Giovanni* and *Fidelio*. The opera seria, however, is still part of feudal, courtly ceremonial. On the other hand, the opera buffa, as is quite clear in Pergolesi, belongs to the bourgeois opposition. Wagner united the two under the primacy of the bourgeoisie, which in exchange renounced any far-reaching oppositional impulse. This is precisely registered by the *parlando*. In the late works we find that the *parlando* of the *Liebesverbot* has abandoned its ironic character, its ability to unmask the dignity of the rulers—the quality that had actually earned it its reputation for wit. Instead it deserts irony for pathos, and the bellowing of Wagnerian singers is the child of this *mésalliance*. This bourgeoisified pathos—the phrase suggests why it verges on the ludicrous—creates its own linguistic device in Wagner in his use of alliteration. This is related to the progressive tendency in prose. Just as the music divests itself of all stereotypes, so too it is reluctant to tolerate them in the text. The bourgeois in opposition campaigns for the disenchantment of language. The impotent deserter, however, strives atavistically to wrest a new form of magic from the disenchantment: bourgeois language should sound as if Being itself were being made to speak. As a progressive, Wagner transformed the language of verse so that it no longer interfered with the musical intonation and fitted as snugly as prose to both thought and music. As a reactionary, he mixed in a magic ingredient and performed a linguistic gesture that simulated a condition existing before the division into prose and verse.

In general, Wagner's music adopts an original attitude towards language. He does not respond to it, nor does he roam around the woods and caverns of the word like Schubert. Instead language, as the interpreter of its allegorical images, the leitmotivs, is filtered through its wire-mesh, as if it were a foreign object. Wagner's success in this is due to a stratum of experience that has been little noticed: to the capacity to assimilate things that are themselves thing-like, prosaic, dry and unmusical. In the characterization of Beckmesser and Mime the frontiers of expression are pushed back well beyond poetic subjectivity, without lapsing into mere illustration; in this Wagner comes closest to a composer completely unknown to him: Mussorgsky. With the high style expanding and spreading itself out over the meanness of quotidian reality and over a world already becoming 'bourgeois' in the negative sense, completely new musical characters were crystallized. The further development of this tendency more than any other is what gave Hugo Wolf his particular tone; it perished at the hands of Strauss's witticisms. The same Wagner whose foible was the moulding of purely musical characters, is unsurpassed in his gift for translating expressive characters into music. They then form part of the complexion of his entire musical language. The exhortation of the hero of Bayreuth, 'Children, create something new!', may well proclaim the demand for such new expressive characters. In actuality, with the single exception of Mahler, they atrophied after Wagner himself, sacrificed in favour of immanent compositional techniques, and the withering of this faculty has undoubtedly something to do with the specialist nature of modern music in its outstanding representatives. But this faculty, which always leaves itself time for amplification, is by no means dramatic in nature, and in fact Wagner's talent was primarily theatrical rather than dramatic. The strange genre-attributions of the works from *Tristan* on—*The Mastersingers* is not assigned to any genre— suggest that Wagner himself was not unaware of this. He seems too ideological for the drama: he is unable to make the idea take second place to the action and to speak simply through the action, but feels instead that as an artist he must also play the part of the apologist who has to make his statement directly. He shares with the Romantic movement a tendency towards epic: in the act of reporting the prehistoric world his music salutes it. It sometimes even adopts the diction of a reporter, as we see, for example, in Act III of *Siegfried* where Siegfried learns what fear is in the scene with the sleeping Brünnhilde. The feelings expressed are not, above all in the late works, those of the dramatis personae, but those of the reflecting author. Considered as a musical function, however, this serves to cancel time. Wotan's lengthy narratives in Act II of *The Valkyrie*, or Siegfried's just before his death, have no dramatic justification. They provide nothing that could not have taken place in the action itself. But at decisive points in the drama—Wotan's denial of the will and the destruction of the one great hope—they deflect the action itself back into the past, just as the formal meaning of the gesture of the 'Bar'-form was its self-cancellation and return to the body. The Wagnerian narratives call a halt to the action and hence, too, to the life process of society. They cause it to stand still so as to accompany it down into the kingdom of death, the ideal of Wagnerian music. The fact that it functions as an accompaniment is what gives Wagner's music its epic character. As it draws its heroes along with it, in joy or sorrow, it anticipates the verdict of society. But the more eager it is to commend itself to the audience as if it were their own decision, the more it must pretend to be directly identical with its figures, identical on this side of the divide between singer and hero. For this reason the talking poet in the costume of the 'Master' must insist on his mythic identity with his own creatures and, acting as the actor of his characters, must imitate them musically. This explains the ambiguity of his musical stance; it confuses the lyrical reflectiveness of the dramatic personage and the gestural and emotional directness of the conductor. Something of this is expressed in the letter to Liszt in which Wagner tells him that he has interrupted work on the *Ring*, saying that he had led his young Siegfried to the linden tree and there taken leave of him with many heartfelt tears.[4]

[4] See the letter of 28 June 1857 in the *Correspondence of Wagner and Liszt*, trans. F. Hueffer, New York 1969 (reprint), Vol. 2, p. 204.

The tears that his music sheds over its own children are meant in reality for the man who sheds them. In letting itself be moved by him, the public is meant to welcome the penitent prodigal son. The common meeting-ground is not reconciliation in a common life but the deadly fate to which they have both fallen prey.

4
Sonority

The contradictions underlying the formal and melodic structure of Wagner's music—the necessary precondition of the failure at the level of technique—may generally be located in the fact that eternal sameness presents itself as the eternally new, the static as the dynamic, or that, conversely, intrinsically dynamic categories are projected onto unhistorical, pre-subjective characters. Wagner's composition is inconsistent, but not because it aims at stasis or at Being in the sense of the ontological ideology of the middle of the twentieth century, along the lines of Stravinsky. Despite a profound affinity in their concern with the prehistoric, or perhaps even because of it, Stravinsky regards himself as the complete antipode of Wagner. Stravinsky is inexhaustible in finding new forms for regression; in his aesthetic ideology, as in the ideology of Fascism, the concept of progress is repudiated. Wagner, however, living a century earlier and rooted in a liberalism whose own atavism he anticipated, would like to present the regressive element as progress, the static as the dynamic. For he was the exponent of a class that was already threatened by historical tendencies, without yet feeling itself to be condemned by history. Instead it projected the foreseeable end of its own dynamism onto the ground of Being as a metaphysical catastrophe. And in fact the atavistic moments in Wagner are always ones in which productive forces are set free. The individual subject who is affected now for the first time in music by the crisis in society, does not just benefit infinitely, despite his weakness, in terms of concrete richness, expressiveness and subtlety. In addition, when compared to the would-be sovereign individual of the age of bourgeois ascendancy, he exhibits other features, such as a willingness to let himself go and a refusal to harden out and keep himself to himself—features that point beyond the order to which he belongs.

Nowhere do these aspects of Wagner blossom more happily than where his regressive tendency is free from the lie of being dynamic; where, as it were, the social subject can look its own atavism in the face musically and write its history by incorporating it in its material without distortion. For this reason the really productive element in Wagner is seen at the moments when the subject abdicates sovereignty and passively abandons itself to the archaic, the instinctual—the element which, precisely because it has been emancipated, renounces its now unattainable claim to give meaningful shape to the passage of time. This element, with its two dimensions of harmony and colour, is sonority. Through sonority, time seems transfixed in space, and while as harmony it 'fills' space, the notion of colour, for which musical theory has no better name, is directly borrowed from the realm of visual space. At the same time it is mere sonority which actually represents that unarticulated natural state into which Wagner dissolves. But if in Wagner music does regress to the non-temporal medium of sound, the latter's own remoteness from time allows it to develop largely unhindered by the tendencies that constantly paralyse its structures within the time-dimension. It is as expressiveness that the subjective force of production makes its boldest advances at the level of harmony: inventions like the sleep-motiv in the *Ring* resemble magic spells that are capable of enticing all subsequent harmonic discoveries from the twelve-tone continuum. Wagner's anticipation of impressionism in his use of harmony is even more striking than in his tendency towards atomization. The familiar examples from *Tristan* can be augmented by a number of extreme cases: *The Valkyrie* develops whole-tone complexes out of augmented triads; in *Siegfried*, just before Mime's words, 'Your mother gave me this', there is an implicit, if not harmonically literal, polytonal passage that hovers between C major and F minor. Above all, however, we should remind ourselves here of the tritonal base of the short scene between the Wanderer and Fafner and much of that between Fafner and Siegfried, where the concept of harmonic movement is suspended, exactly in the Debussyan sense, and is replaced by the shifting around of functionally equivocal cords. Despite this it would be a mistake to interpret Wagner's use of harmony without further ado as impressionism. We must of course not forget that Renoir did his portrait, but if he rejected impressionism in painting—the same impressionism whose techniques were later transferred to music by Debussy—there can still be no doubt as to the meaning of his praise of Titian at the expense of modern 'daubers'. There is no mistaking Wagner's playful inclination, in all matters outside his own narrow area of competence, to take the side of authoritarian classicism against the 'moderns': Nietzsche's idea of Wagner as a man out of key with his time was distorted into spiteful self-righteousness in the author of *Tristan*, the idol of the Paris symbolists down to Mallarmé. At the same time, however, his own harmonic innovations lead well beyond the impressionism at least of his own successors. Whereas Richard Strauss employed the Wagnerian dissonances, and the dissonances developed out of them, merely to titillate, inserting them in massive clusters into a primitive harmonic structure far less advanced than Wagner's, the older composer uses the new chords on occasion in such a way as to undermine the basic scheme. They gain in constructive power. Even at the level of detail his dissonances go well beyond those of impressionism. In Wotan's great outburst in *The Valkyrie*, just before the words 'O sacred disgrace', there is a chord containing six different pitch classes (C, F, A♭, D♭, C♭, D) that is never actually resolved. And in *Siegfried*—at Mime's words, 'And for all my worry/this is now my reward'—there is a ninth chord that is just as dissonant. In the two last operas the pentachord of the diminished seventh with superposed minor ninth acquires the significance of a leitmotiv; this is particularly crass when, as often in *Parsifal*, it is continued by being arpeggiated in one voice instead of with a resolution.[1] However, more important than the mere occurrence of such sounds is their function. The customary interpretation, which is based on the concepts of diatonic semitonal steps, chromaticism and enharmony, misses the point. In origin, the increasing Romantic tendency towards chromaticism was progressive. In Wagner's hands, within a system totally

---

[1] Adorno seems to be thinking of Kundry's scream. *Translator's note.*

dominated by semitone steps, without any opposing force, it
becomes for the first time somehow bland and static. But even here
counter-forces are released: precisely as a totality the chromaticism
generates resistances within itself, vigorous secondary triads that
by no means just replace the tonic and the dominant. Kurth in
particular has failed to do this justice. He did of course notice the
emancipation of the dissonance from its resolution and the
fundamental process whereby what was previously inessential had
now become autonomous.[2] But at the same time he thinks of the
dissonances as 'pure sound effects' instead of seeing them also as
hierarchically related harmonies, and thereby forms an exact
theoretical parallel to Strauss's practice of dissonant clusters.[3] It is
not for nothing that the concept of the sound effect became one of
the shoddiest journalistic clichés of the first decades of the
twentieth century. Kurth would undoubtedly not want any truck
with this. His interpretation of harmony as 'energetic' and not just
as sound seems to belong to an avant-garde vocabulary and helps
to give an insight into what is in principle the dynamic character of
harmony. Kurth interpreted the harmonic relationship between
dissonance and consonance as one of tension and resolution. With
the concept of tension between harmonic events to replace that of a
merely static registration of their occurrence within the figured bass
notation, the vestiges of obsolete theoretical schemes are
liquidated, schemes which, anyway, had already come under
attack from Riemann's concept of function. But according to
Kurth the tensions merely conceal and paraphrase the resolution
'for' which they stand and in and by which they are determined.
He therefore deprives the notion of tension of its seminal value,
and despite all the subjective and psychological turns of phrase, or
perhaps rather for their sake, clings to the concept of the
'nonharmonic' inherited from the repertoire of the conservatory.
He overlooks the fact that the 'dissonances' of, say, the 'Tristan'
chord have been so distributed as to become the main thing. In
Wagner's phrasing the dissonances have assumed the character of
sovereign subjectivity vis-à-vis the resolutions: they protest against

[2] Cf. Kurth, p. 297 f.
[3] Cf. ibid., p. 302 f.

the right of a social authority to make the rules. All the energy is on the side of the dissonance; in comparison the individual resolutions become increasingly threadbare, superfluous decor or conservative protestation. Tension is made into an absolute principle by ensuring that, as in a giant credit system, the negation of the negation, the full settlement of debt, is indefinitely postponed. By ignoring this, by forcing the dissonances to bow to the consonance that they contradict and which is only outwardly a match for them, Kurth through his very benevolence towards the 'modern' dynamic aspect of harmony nevertheless manages to smuggle in a traditionalist and authoritarian element. And wherever the actual dissonances make a mockery of such an interpretation Kurth is forced to degrade them to the level of mere tonal effects, something that had been contradicted by his own vigorous criticism of the concept of sonority. Only very occasionally, in his treatment of the opposing theories of harmony of Riemann and Sechter, does he come closer to a dialectical interpretation of Romantic harmony.[4] Apart from that, he remains unable to break out of an undialectical, functional view of harmony.

Of course, Wagner himself encourages this with his famous definition of music as the art of transition,[5] and the tendency towards an allegorical return to unarticulated nature ultimately justifies him. The impulse to invalidate anything with a definite shape, to make everything flow and to obliterate every clear frontier is translated technically into a concern for constant mediation. But functionality, the mediation of tension and resolution that has no use for any surplus, for anything left outside the process—this method must not be construed too crudely, too literally or short-sightedly. Wagner's harmonic practice is by no means exhausted by the concept of transition. We are not thinking here of diatonicism as such, which Lorenz mobilizes as a facile retort to Kurth. But in The Mastersingers, which is largely diatonic, the archaic stylization, very closely analogous to Brahms's modality, permits that reinforcement of the secondary triads

[4] Cf. ibid., pp. 308n, 311.
[5] Wagner, letter of 29 October 1859, to Mathilde Wesendonk; quoted by Kurth, p. 454n.

which limits the primacy of the dominant and simultaneously enriches tonality; the old-fashioned becomes the leaven of the modern. However, the weightiest consequence of this counter-tendency, the process by which the harmonic detail becomes autonomous, is precisely the emancipation of the dissonance from its various resolutions. This process is highlighted by accentuation. In the progressive harmonic sections, the accents fall consistently on the dissonances, not the resolutions. In *Parsifal*, which begins to subject all purely ornamental elements of music to criticism, the dissonances sometimes emerge openly as the victors, they burst the conventions of resolution and are 'resolved' instead into bare single lines. When Wagner expressed the opinion that Parsifal's cry, 'Amfortas!—the wound!', exceeded in its power Tristan's curse of love, he placed eight bars in the centre of his work which in their whole structure are poised immediately on the threshold of atonality. But no closer than the threshold. Wagner's ambiguity determines even the Janus-quality of his harmony. This, together with the emancipation of dissonance, not only intensifies the expression but also extends its realm. Ambiguity itself becomes an element of expression. In Beethoven and well into high Romanticism the expressive values of harmony are fixed: dissonance stands for negation and suffering, consonance for fulfilment and the positive. In Wagner this is changed in the direction of a greater subjective differentiation of the emotional values of harmony. To illustrate, we may think of the characteristic chord with the allegorical rubric 'Spring's command, sweet necessity' in *The Mastersingers*, which represents the element of erotic passion and hence summarizes the whole action. It tells both of the poignant pain of non-fulfilment and of the pleasure that lies in the tension: it is both sweet and necessary. This intermediate stratum of expression, which is indeed the epitome of the musical modernity of the nineteenth century, did not exist before Wagner. That suffering can be sweet, and that the poles of pleasure and pain are not rigidly opposed to one another, but are mediated, is something that both composers and audience learned uniquely from him, and it is this experience alone that made it possible for dissonance to extend its range over the whole language of music. And few aspects of Wagner's music have been as seductive as the enjoyment of pain.

But whereas dissonance is regularly deployed in the mature works as the bearer of expression, its actual expressive value continues to exploit the contrast with the triad; the chords are expressive not in any absolute way but only in their implied distance from consonance, by which they are measured even where consonance is omitted. In the overall conception, the supremacy of tonality remains unchallenged, and to apply the concept of progress in harmony everywhere in Wagner where novel chord patterns appeared would be to take an over-simple view of the matter. Wagner no more deviates significantly from the dominant musical idiom than he does from the immanent reality of bourgeois society, and his innovations are largely absorbed into the tradition, however much their ultimate effect is to undermine it. Wagner's achievements have modified the language of music only indirectly, by extending tonal space, rather than directly, by suspending it. Despite Lorenz's eulogies of the key plan of entire acts and works, their influence on the organization of his work is astonishingly slight. The absence of any real thematic construction also affects his use of harmony. Riemann's 'functions' are indeed everywhere, but there is no 'functional harmony' in the sense given to it in Schoenberg's theory; no general formal perspective is produced by the disposition either of individual events or of the equivocal harmony. Wagner's distaste for modulation, this strange conservative residue that fits in so easily with the technique of mere semitonal side-stepping, ends up by depriving his harmony of its best resource, that of a formal organization in depth of the kind that Bruckner, that so much clumsier pupil of Sechter, attempted on the surface. On the occasions when Wagner does not make up his mind to modulate for once, in order, as in the overture to *The Mastersingers*, to break free from the all too persistent key of C major, his use of modulation, which never quite escapes from the sense of side-stepping, seems peculiarly arbitrary, unbalanced and is so abrupt as always to be on the verge of losing its formal balance with the lengthier scalic passages that precede it; from all of which it of course extracts stimuli for further effects. The limits of Wagnerian form are also those of his harmony.

Inseparably from the other elements of his mode of composition, his harmony is also implicated in the contradictions of his style. What I have in mind primarily here is a fact whose full significance is still unappreciated, namely that his mature works, even where the orchestration is at its richest, are always based on an almost academic adherence to the four-voice harmonic texture. Very often this has the following form: melody in the top voice—sustained bass with changing significance—the inner voices give harmonic support or glide chromatically. The four-voice harmonic texture is explicable in terms of the excessive respect of the outsider-cum-dilettante for the regular 'chorale' of harmonic theory, but perhaps also of the stance of a time-beating composer. The chorale provides the harmonic unfolding of the regular pulse, in which a chord falls at each beat. The Wanderer harmonies in *Siegfried* provide a model of this. A harmonic monotony corresponds to the metrical monotony at least inasmuch as this scheme is scarcely varied: the harmonies and their relationship, but not the harmonization, are permeated by Wagner's emancipatory intentions and it might often appear as if by the textbook setting of chords that break all the rules the harmonic revolutionary were anxious to placate the teachers he had escaped. The harmonic texture is flattened out by the use of the bass pedals: in general there are fewer bass notes than harmonic events. This gives rise to a certain ponderousness, the characteristic viscous flow of his music. This is doubtless the legacy of his dilettantish paucity of scale degrees in his youth, as in the Allegro–non-tanto prelude just before Rienzi's 'Adriano, you? A Colonna?'. Out of this necessity the mature Wagner made the virtue of harmonic polyvalence. The enharmonic element acquires a highly paradoxical significance. This can be understood better from its prehistory than from the end-product in *Tristan*. It can already be seen in the overture to the *Flying Dutchman* in which the modulation from D minor to A♭ major is effected by changing the meaning of a diminished seventh chord initially related to A minor. *Lohengrin* has it in a fully developed form in Elsa's vision, with those eight bars which Wagner himself cited as paradigmatic, which modulate from A♭ major, through C♭ major, B minor, D major, D minor, F major-minor and back to A♭ major. The point here is the enharmonic change of the C♭ to B, which, moreover, comes off as the unexpected, the Berliozian *imprévu*. In *Rienzi* this surprise effect, for example that of the G♭ after the sentence, 'that I hold you to be noble, free and great!', still disrupts the whole texture brutally and crassly. Later on, in the *Lohengrin* passage, it is integrated enharmonically into the whole composition. The new is simultaneously the old: in the new it recognizes itself again and becomes easy to grasp.

'It sounded so old, and yet was so new'[6]

— that could be the rule presiding over Wagner's enharmonics and that of his harmony as a whole. Chords like that on the first beat of the third bar of *The Mastersingers* overture, the Tristan chord or the chord of the Rhinemaidens in *Twilight of the Gods* that accompanies their warning to Siegfried, can be traced back to the 'old', to concepts like transition, alteration and suspension. But, by a strange reversal of the norm, these devices come to occupy the centre of the musical process and this endows them with an unprecedented power. They become fully comprehensible only in the light of a comparison with the most advanced material of contemporary music from which the inexorable presence of the Wagnerian transition has been eliminated.

---

[6] Hans Sachs in *The Mastersingers*, Act II, sc. 3. *Translator's note.*

5
Colour

Whereas Wagnerian harmony swings between past and future, the
dimension of colour is, properly speaking, his own discovery. The
art of orchestration in the precise sense, as the productive share of
colour in the musical process 'in such a way that colour itself
becomes action',[1] is something that did not exist before Wagner.
He was the first to make subtle compositional nuances tangible and
to render the unity of compositional complexes by colouristic
methods. Richard Strauss remarks in his new edition of Berlioz's
Treatise on Instrumentation that each work of Wagner's had its own
combination of instruments, its own orchestral style, and that
Wagner's talent for instrumental stylization was so far developed
that, even within the overarching unity of the *Ring*, each of the
four operas had its own distinct quality of sound. The Wagnerian
art of instrumentation has caught up with the harmonic arts of
blending and transition, without being bound to older techniques
such as diatonicism. In comparison the achievement of Berlioz was
external and mechanical. He did, it is true, discover how to create
luminous orchestral effects as well as the values of the individual
colours, but he did not bring these colouristic discoveries to the
composition as such, or make use of them in a compositionally
productive way. If Wagner learns about the emancipation of
colour from line from Berlioz, his own achievement is to win back
the liberated colour for line and to abolish the old distinction
between them. Here he gains a signal victory over conventional
schemes of every kind. Just as it is the case that there was no art of

[1] *Richard Wagner's Prose Works*, Vol. 3, p. 330.

orchestration before Wagner, it is no less true that to this day it has not been possible to devise a canonic theory of orchestration to match the theory of harmony and counterpoint. All we can offer are classifications of timbres and empirical advice. There is no rule governing the choice of colour; it can prove itself only in terms of the concrete requirements of the specific context, something which was established for harmony and above all melody only in contemporary music. The colouristic dimension, a realm where Wagner is completely at home, is in the first instance the domain of his subjectivity, and the colouristic sensibility of Wagner the orchestrator is the complement to the sensual susceptibility of the man who wrote the letters to the milliner.[2] For all his expansion of the apparatus of instrumentation and for all his development of autonomous technique, Wagner's orchestra is essentially intimate: the composer who fled to the conductor's rostrum is only really at home in the orchestra, where the voices of the instruments address him, magical and familiar at the same time, as colours are to children. And in fact the authentic conception of Wagner's orchestral art does coincide with his turning towards the intimate in *Lohengrin*. Strauss, to whom we owe the only useful pointers to the theory of Wagnerian instrumentation, urgently counsels the student to study the finer points of woodwind combination in that opera. Neither the *Dutchman* nor *Tannhäuser* contains any great instrumental intuitions. The principle of combination as structurally significant does not appear until *Lohengrin*.

The particular place of the woodwinds and woodwind combinations in *Lohengrin* is linked to the poetic idea of the wedding that dictates the style of the entire opera, and not just the bridal procession and the nuptial chamber. Strauss has drawn attention at one point to the imitation of the sound of the organ as a way of allegorizing that poetic idea: use of the organ itself implies the task of reconciling the orchestral sound with the sound of the organ, which is alien to Grand Opera and indeed unbearably banal within it. This leads to the combination of highly contradictory elements. The minister and lady's bower of medieval romance give rise to

[2] Wagner's letters to Bertha Goldwag, a Viennese milliner, were first published in 1906. An English translation by Sophie Prombaum, *Richard Wagner and the Seamstress*, appeared in New York, 1941. *Translator's note.*

the use of the organ to evoke the ideal image of an all-embracing cosmos confirmed by God, and the woodwinds create this archaic picture. Their task is, as it were, to present an objective counterweight to the subjective expressiveness of the strings. At the same time, however, in the name of that desire for a seamless formal totality which constitutes the substance of Wagner's polemic against the traditional opera, the woodwinds must be harmonized as closely as possible with the sound of the strings in which they must indeed be wholly merged. Strauss speaks of the 'cementing' function of the woodwinds. By imitating the organ, their organ-like inflexibility is softened. The models for their mixed sounds are provided on the one hand by the combinations of organ-stops, on the other by the blending, merging possibilities of the string sections.

Insight into this and into the function of Wagner's orchestration in general can be acquired only from an analysis of this work, which is of such crucial importance for his conception of the orchestra. At the beginning of Act I, scene 2, the words, 'See, she comes to answer her heavy charge!',[3] are followed by eight-bars of wind writing. Thematically, the sentence is closely related to the enharmonic passage in Elsa's narration of her dream. It is divided into two four-beat bars. In the antecedent the woodwind parts are doubled throughout, even when playing *piano*. The immediate explanation of this is the need to correct a certain lack of homogeneity. The flutes are both less penetrating and also harder to fuse than the clarinets; they are too feeble and at the same time they do not harmonize with the overall colouring. But equally, in terms of the subtle critique of sound carried out by Wagner's instrumentation, the oboes are used as doubling instruments only in *forte*. In *piano* passages their timbre is, as it were, too penetrating, too narrow in its expressive radius, to be mistaken for anything but that of the oboe; if they are combined with flutes in unison, they dominate instead of merging with them. Negatively, the changed use of the oboes is one of Wagner's most important innovations. In the traditional score the oboes are placed above the clarinets and in Viennese Classicism they are for the most part pitched higher as

[3] *Lohengrin, kleine Partitur*, ed. Breitkopf & Härtl, Leipzig 1906, p. 55 f.

well. Taken together with the colourlessness of the clarinets, this gives rise to that striking lack of balance and arbitrariness of the sound combinations in the classical woodwind chorus that Wagner found so unbearable. It was because of this that his use of the oboes was limited on principle either to the solo or the *forte tutti*, but he no longer employed them automatically as the natural second soprano in the wind section. In the antecedent of that *Lohengrin* sentence, the conclusion that he draws from his critique of the flute sound on the one hand and the oboe on the other, is to use clarinets to double both the flute melody in the top voice and the second soprano part which is also played by the flute. But this doubling is not designed simply for additional emphasis, any more than the *piano* doubling of the strings in Beethoven. On the contrary, its function is to change the tone colour. The unison combination of flute and clarinet gives rise to floating, oscillating acoustic 'beats'. In it the specific sound of each instrument is lost; they can no longer be separated out, and the final sound gives no clue as to how it was created. In this it resembles the thing-like sound of the organ. But at the same time—and this is highly symptomatic of the dual nature of Wagner's orchestration—such a process of objectification has advantages in terms of a greater flexibility for the whole. Any loss in individual timbre sustained by the single instrument as a result of doubling is made up for by the possibility of smooth integration with the orchestra as a whole. No doubt it is less able to assert its own individual character, but if the partial, subjective performances of the players are absorbed into the overall effect, it is equally true that the latter in turn becomes the willing medium of the expression the composer wishes to exact. The more reification, the more subjectivity: the maxim holds good in orchestration as in epistemology. If the clarinets cancel out the archaic irrationality of the flutes, the bass clarinet lends support to the bassoon, the old-fashioned and retrograde member of the woodwinds. Henceforth this is consigned to the *tutti* or else is reserved for special effects, such as Mime's thirds. As the bass of that wind chorus,[4] the third bassoon is doubled by the bass clarinet; the first is doubled in unison with the third flute, usually as an inner

---

[4] Ibid., p. 35.

pedal whose stasis is supported by its no doubt intentional lack of instrumental character. The simultaneous merging of the instruments to achieve a balanced timbre is matched by the orchestrating-out of transitions by means of a technique of instrumental 'residues' which is not only intensified to the heights of virtuosity in *Tristan*, but also remains the rule in Schoenberg and, above all, Alban Berg. The relation between antecedent and consequent in that *Lohengrin* period provides an instructive basic model of this. The two are so intimately intertwined that the entry of the consequent on a fresh group of instruments—two oboes, English horn and the hitherto unused second bassoon—coincides with the end of the antecedent. The latter is entrusted wholly to the flutes, while the instruments that had been doubled in unison with them until then, two clarinets and the first bassoon, now fall silent. The effect of this is that a 'residue' of the previous sound enters into the new one, without any hiatus. And it is the less prominent part of the previous sound, the part that had no independent existence, that functions as this residue. This is reinforced by the dynamics of the passage, since the flutes fade away in *piano* whereas the new group enters likewise in *piano*. At the moment when the instruments change over the flutes merge so completely with the oboes and the English horn that what we hear is not so much an actual 'entry' as a mere timbral inflexion. In this way the antecedent and consequent are cemented together in a transition as slight as the melodic minor third in which the consequent is joined to the antecedent, from which it nevertheless remains distinct. Thus the orchestration is transformed into an integral feature of the composition. However disguised, the relationship between antecedent and consequent is basically that of *tutti* to solo. The antecedent makes a great imploring gesture; the consequent withdraws into itself in tones of acceptance. In the antecedent there is both crescendo and diminuendo, in the consequent diminuendo alone. If the expression of this relationship had been entrusted solely to the dynamics of playing, it would have been lost as the result of the inevitable coarsening effect of the theatre on all music. It becomes effective as a result of the instrumentation itself. Because of the doubling, the antecedent has the effect of a *tutti*; it is played by eight instruments, whereas the consequent makes do, initially, with four. But Wagner goes even further. The formal meaning of the antecedent-consequent relationship is actualized by the choice of instrumental timbres. The solo timbre of the oboe displaces the 'beats' of flute and clarinet. In a sense it stands midway between the flute, with which it shares an archaic pastoral quality, and the clarinet, whose timbre it approaches in the register in question. The oboe does not possess the wavery solitariness of the flute, but neither is it as gregarious as the clarinet, and its pastoral note is that of an innocence that is waiting to be released. For this reason the oboe, which is itself ambiguous, is the predestined heir to the foregoing ambiguous 'beats', without contrasting too abruptly with them. For both as music and as gesture the entire period forms a unity and because of the great time-span involved, Wagner can make only the most sparing use of stark instrumental contrasts. Hence the use of the flute chord as a cement. At the same time, however, the oboe has a solo effect, simply because it is not doubled. Its timbre is appropriate to the gesture of modesty of the consequent, of which Wagner's stage-direction speaks. With a minimal variation in timbre and a strict avoidance of all external contrasts, the antecedent-consequent relationship of *tutti* to solo is able to establish itself in the most economical way with the transfer from flute and clarinet to the oboe. The orchestration adds a new dimension to the bare symmetry of antecedent and consequent and detaches the eight-bar period from its framework. The latent intention of the form is orchestrated out. Had Wagner wished to achieve the same end without the help of the orchestration it would have placed too much strain on the smaller components of the period. The function of the orchestral setting follows logically from the economy of the composition as a whole.

The simultaneous combination of flute and clarinet prevents the listener from perceiving how they were produced; their specific character is obscured and they vanish in an enchanted sound that appears unrelated to any instrumental grouping. This pheno-menon touches on a basic feature of Wagner's orchestration, which appears most clearly in his treatment of the horn. The central importance of the horn in the Wagnerian orchestra was pointed out by Richard Strauss. As the main element in fanfares and flourishes it was always, long before Beethoven, a gestural instrument. In Wagner it assumes an expressive function, parallel to the orchestral gesture of *accompagnato* recitative. This change in function becomes apparent with the replacement of the natural horn, which was confined to the diatonic scale, by the valve-horn, on which the chromatic scale could be played. Even though the valve-horn had been invented in Wagner's childhood, it is evident that he could bring himself to introduce it only with great reluctance. In a note on the score of *Tristan* he remarks: 'It is indisputable that the introduction of valves has brought such great gain for this instrument that it is difficult to ignore this improvement, even though as a result the horn has undeniably lost something of its beauty of tone, and above all its ability to connect the notes smoothly. In view of this great loss the composer who is concerned to preserve the true character of the horn would have to abstain from using the valve-horn, were it not for the fact, which is also vouchsafed by experience, that outstanding artists who handle their instruments with care are able to eliminate the disadvantages that have been mentioned almost without a trace, so that scarcely any distinction in tone and linkage could be detected.' These sentences confirm Newman's remark that Wagner always speaks perfectly sensibly of purely musical matters and becomes irresponsible only when he goes beyond the limits of his own experience, limits drawn by the division of labour he so abhorred. His Romantic outlook does not prevent him from seeing that the process of rationalization that threatens 'true character' also releases the forces—the forces of conscious men—that compensate for such 'disadvantages'. He is far superior to that phrase about 'the loss of substance' which is used at a later stage of rationalization to dismiss the entire process, a rejection of rationalization which only makes things easier for those who administer it. At the same time, Wagner, like the critics of political economy, was under no illusions about the price that had to be paid for progress. No one who has ever heard a natural horn and a valve-horn, one after the other, will be inclined to question where the 'true character' of the horn whose loss he mourns is to be found. It is in the trace that lingers on in the horn of the way in which the note has been produced. A note 'sounds like a horn' as long as you can still hear that it has been played on the horn: its origin, together with the risk of a false note, help to form the quality of the sound. It is this trace that is lost in the valve-horn. Wagner's horns are often compared to piano pedals. We need not intervene here in the dispute over whether Liszt's piano style or Wagner's orchestral style has priority. What is clear is that the difference between the pedalled note and the non-pedalled note on the piano is that in the former the trace of its production, which is heard at the moment when the hammer strikes the string, is eliminated. Something of the same kind happens with the horns, since the use of the valve mechanism alienates them from the immediate production of their own sound. The fact that Wagner's orchestra has various degrees of immediacy is something he owes to the horns. When a number of instruments sound simultaneously, not all are 'there' in equal measure, and not just in the sense that prominent principal voices are contrasted with retiring secondary ones. The fact is that in his case there are fundamental instrumental parts that are indeed perfectly audible, but yet appear to run their course as if beneath the manifest surface of the composition, rather like the different layers of immediacy in a dream. The often veiled, inexplicit tone of the valve-horn has predestined it for such *obligato* parts. Its emancipation from the mode of its production allows it to assume the task of acting as the orchestral 'cement' even more readily than the flexible clarinets. Its loss of 'character' brings it closer to other instrumental timbres which, for their part, draw nearer to the horn and to each other.

The Wagnerian orchestra aims at producing a continuum of timbres and has therefore inaugurated a tendency which has become dominant in our day at the extreme poles of production. On the one hand, in the Schoenberg school, the instruments become interchangeable and lose their crude specificity. On the other, as Alban Berg remarked, the orchestrator must proceed like a carpenter who makes sure that there are no nails sticking out from his table and that there is no smell of glue, and so in jazz, in line with this, muted trumpets sound like saxophones and vice versa, and even the singer who sings in a whisper or through a megaphone sounds not unlike them too. The whole trend is summed up in radical, even mechanical form in the idea of an

(electrical continuum of all possible timbres.)Of course, Wagner attempts to interpret the technological trend as a natural event. He replaces the individual instruments of the orchestra with the idea of instrumental 'families', such as the clarinets or the tubas, which then enter into relationships that he thinks of as elective affinities. There is indeed something in the idea that Wagner's orchestration is inseparable from the idea of the human body: some of his theatrical figures seem to be instruments of the orchestra that have become flesh and blood. It is easy to imagine, for example, that the contrasts in Kundry's character have arisen from those in the clarinet register of which her themes are so reminiscent, even though they are only occasionally presented by the clarinet. But the discovery of the productive imaginative power of timbre is not without its negative effects on composition. The appearance, which in Wagner nourishes the essence, if it does not indeed create it, is also the side that the work of art presents to the world, in other words, it is the 'effect'. Not only does the appearance become the essence, but inevitably the essence becomes appearance; the integration of the different elements takes place at the expense of the integrity of the composition. In his idiosyncratic resistance to naked instrumental sound whose origins are readily discernible, Wagner doubles the instruments—and doubling in unison is the *Ur*-phenomenon of Wagner's blended timbres. But the very fact of this doubling introduces something superfluous, false and dressed-up into the orchestration, something that interferes with the unity of composition and orchestral sound, even though it was in order to achieve this unity that he had extended the art of orchestration. Even in Wagner, to' say nothing of the Neo-Germans, there is a tendency towards over-orchestration, a tendency to represent events as more than they musically are. This sometimes results in palpable divergences of timbre from construction, above all in his use of 'padding-voices'. These are a product of the tendency to blend the instruments and to achieve a seamless representation in sound of the structure of the composition, but they are not identical with this and assume instead a spurious autonomy too explicit for harmony and too amorphous for counterpoint. The much-lauded 'simplicity' of the orchestration in

Parsifal is, therefore, not just reactionary or marked by a false religiosity, as compared with *Tristan, The Mastersingers* and the *Ring*. The fact is rather that it carries out a legitimate critique of the ornamental components in Wagner's characteristic style of orchestration. Thus it contains not just the religiose brass choirs but also something of the bleak austerity of sound that was to become dominant in Mahler's last works and subsequently in the Viennese School. In art the ascetic ideal is dialectical. Nowadays, clothed in matter-of-fact garb, it mainly serves the cause of obscurantism and rancour towards happiness, whether of the senses or the intellect. Its other side is its subversion of the aesthetic appearance. This helps to make good the promise of art by eliminating the illusory fulfilment in aesthetic form and enabling its own negativity to express the contradiction between the real and the possible.

The achievements of Wagnerian orchestration are not confined to the wind instruments. Strauss speaks of Wagner's *al fresco* treatment of the strings in the Fire Music, which contains figures that can no longer be played precisely in time by a single violin and which yet 'resound' in the chorus because there the inadequacies of individual playing disappear. The massed use of strings provided Wagner with the model for the innovations he made in the use of wind combinations. He was not the first to have given them such prominence. Even earlier the classical orchestra had purchased its comprehensiveness, its grasp of a total process by sacrificing individual spontaneities among the string players, and with it what we may think of as the natural form of sound. With Wagner it becomes a metaphor of infinity by curtailing the finite achievements of which it is constituted, and the idea of its universal humanity obliterates the traces of living labour, of the individual human being. It may be that the idiosyncratic distaste of composers in the Wagnerian tradition for the naked sound of the solo instrument from amidst the orchestra is the fear of being reminded of this and of the element of injustice implicit in the totality itself. Schreker has provided the clearest expression of this idiosyncrasy in an article published in 1919 in *Anbruch*. 'Nothing is more disruptive than when a celesta, for example, forces itself on my attention . . . I reject . . . its all-too-evident and distinguishable sound . . . and would only recognize one instrument in the service of the opera: the orchestra itself.'[5] The fashionable call in more recent years for an orchestration that did justice to the available material and avoided blends and structurally misleading combinations has tended less to overcome this distaste than to drown it out in the name of honesty. But its overall effect has been to lower the level of orchestration. Justifiable though this protest may have been, it was swiftly transformed into a Pharisaical philistinism that spelt the downfall of the barely won art of orchestration. The artistic ear has rightly rebelled against a string section so weak that it is possible to hear the individual violins. The orchestra is able to suggest transcendental distance by virtue of the concerted neutralization of the individual bowing in the *tutti*.

The key to the theory of the Wagnerian orchestra, which raises such tendencies to the level of a principle, is provided by an understanding of its prehistory. In this respect the massed use of the strings is perhaps less crucial than the classical doubling of the strings by the wind instruments which already have a linking function in *piano*. Such doublings had undoubtedly already existed in the old continuo, where their task was to relate the diverging instruments to the overall harmonic unity. In Haydn and Mozart, however, it is not just unity in diversity that is important, but also diversity in unity. From then on, the fact that different instruments like violins and flutes, or cellos and bassoons, play the same thing, assumes a new significance in the organization of the whole. The traditional reply, which relates the connected sound to the continuousness of the crescendo practised by the Mannheim School, is insufficient, since the Mozartian style is not at all concerned with continuity, but instead places monadic units alongside one another, balances them out and contrasts strings and wind sections in the old concertante manner. Nevertheless, Mozart does favour that particular doubling either at the unison or at the octave. This suggests that it is the naked sound of the single instrument, the bowing of a single violin, the breath of a single horn, that cannot be endured because it conflicts in principle with the orchestral synthesis, just as the single interest of the bourgeois

---

[5] Franz Schreker, *Meine musikdramatische Idee*, reprinted in H.H. Stuckenschmidt, *Neue Musik*, Berlin 1951, p. 357.

individual conflicts with the overall interest of society. The 'subjectivization' of orchestral sound, the transformation of the unruly body of instruments into the docile palette of the composer, is at the same time a de-subjectivization, since its tendency is to render inaudible whatever might give a clue to the origins of a particular sound. If this principle was established in the first instance with the massed use of the strings and did not move on to blending with the wind sections until Wagner, the reason for this lies in the fact that the sounds of inflexible wind instruments do not bear the signs of their subjective production in the same way as the strings; it is not for nothing that the soul-like quality of the violin has been reckoned one of the great innovations of the Cartesian era. The art of the nuance in Wagner's orchestration represents the victory of reification in instrumental practice. The contribution of the immediate subjective production of sound to the aesthetic totality has been displaced in favour of the objective sound available to the composer. The history of Wagner's work, particularly in the dimension of colour, is that of the flight from the banal, by means of which the composer hopes to escape the market requirements of the commodity known as opera. But paradoxically, this flight only leads him more deeply into the commodity. The idea that governs his orchestration, that of sound from which the traces of its production have been removed, sound made absolute, is no more immune to the taint of the commodity than was the trivial sound his art had set out to circumvent. What Schopenhauer says of human life holds good for Wagner's sound, which occupies the same place in the latter's work: 'Certainly human life, like all shoddy goods, is covered over with a false lustre: what suffers always conceals itself.'[6] And this remains true even when it gives expression to suffering.

As a bourgeois art music is young, but with orchestration its latest branch starts to grow. However, it does not arise ready-made, like Athene from the head of Zeus, but repeats in a foreshortened manner the history of music as a whole. Age-old elements of bourgeois praxis come once more to the surface.

[6] Arthur Schopenhauer, *Sämtliche Werke* (Grossherzog Wilhelm Ernst Ausgabe) Vol. 1, *Die Welt als Wille und Vorstellung* I, Leipzig, n.d., p. 431.

Anyone fully able to grasp why Haydn doubles the violins with a
flute in *piano* might well get an intuitive glimpse into why,
thousands of years ago, men gave up eating uncooked grain and
began to bake bread, or why they started to smooth and polish
their tools. Works of art owe their existence to the division of
labour in society, the separation of physical and mental labour. At
the same time, they have their own roots in existence; their
medium is not pure mind, but the mind that enters into reality
and, by virtue of such movement, is able to maintain the unity of
what is divided. It is this contradiction that forces works of art to
make us forget that they have been made. The claim implicit in
their existence and hence, too, the claim that existence has a
meaning, is the more convincing, the less they contain to remind us
that they have been made, and that they owe their being to
something external to themselves, namely to a mental process. Art
that is no longer able to perpetrate this deception with good
conscience has implicitly destroyed the only element in which it
can thrive. This is the case with Wagner: he has lost his good
conscience, but nevertheless his art refuses to relinquish the claim
that it is part of existence in itself. In consequence it is forced to
exaggerate that claim and over-emphasize the natural character of
his work the more, as aesthetic naturalness gives way to reflection
and artifice. In this respect Wagner's oeuvre comes close to the
consumer goods of the nineteenth century which knew no greater
ambition than to conceal every sign of the work that went into
them, perhaps because any such traces reminded people too
vehemently of the appropriation of the labour of others, of an
injustice that could still be felt. A contradiction of all autonomous
art is the concealment of the labour that went into it but in high
capitalism, with the complete hegemony of exchange-value and
with the contradictions arising out of that hegemony, autonomous
art becomes both problematic and programmatic at the same time.
This is the objective explanation for what is generally thought of in
psychological terms as Wagner's mendacity. To make works of art
into magical objects means that men worship their own labour
because they are unable to recognize it as such. It is this that makes
his works pure appearance—an absolutely immediate, as it were,
spatial phenomenon. Not until his late work does he really put

classical aesthetics to the test and when he does he demonstrates its untruth, albeit unwittingly. Because the observer of the work of art is encouraged to adopt a passive role, is relieved of the burden of labour and hence reduced to the mere object of the artistic effect, he is thereby prevented from perceiving the labour that is contained in the work. The work of art endorses the sentiment normally denied by ideology: work is degrading. The concept of work is one from which Wagner has explicitly exempted the artist: 'Apart from the goal of his activity, the artist takes pleasure in the activity itself, in the manipulation and shaping of his material; his production is to him a pleasurable and satisfying activity, not work.'[7] But by the same token, the social isolation of the work of art from its own production is also the measure of its immanent progress, that of its mastery of its own artistic material. All the paradoxes of art in high capitalism—and its very existence is a paradox—culminate in the single paradox that it speaks of the human by virtue of its reification, and that it is only through the perfection of its character as illusion that it partakes of truth.

[7] Carl F. Glasenapp and Heinrich von Stein, *Wagner-Lexikon*, Stuttgart 1883, p. 30.

6

Phantasmagoria

The occultation of production by means of the outward appearance of the product—that is the formal law governing the works of Richard Wagner.[1] The product presents itself as self-producing: hence too the primacy of chromaticism and the leading note. In the absence of any glimpse of the underlying forces or conditions of its production, this outer appearance can lay claim to the status of being. Its perfection is at the same time the perfection of the illusion that the work of art is a reality *sui generis* that constitutes itself in the realm of the absolute without having to renounce its claim to image the world. Wagner's operas tend towards magic delusion, to what Schopenhauer calls 'The outside of the worthless commodity', in short towards phantasmagoria. This is the basis of the

[1] The term 'phantasmagoria' went into German from English, where it was first used in 1802 as the name invented for an exhibition of optical illusions produced chiefly by means of the magic lantern. In this chapter, its negative connotations stem from Marx's use of the word to describe commodity fetishism. Marx argues that the form of the commodity diverges from the commodity itself as a result of the concealment of the fact that the commodity is the product of human labour. 'The commodity-form, and the value relation of the products of labour within which it appears, have absolutely no connection with the physical nature of the commodity and the material relations arising out of this. *It is nothing but a definite social relation between men themselves which assumes here, for them, the phantasmagoric form of a relation between things.*' (*Capital*, Vol. 1, Harmondsworth 1976, p. 165). Marx says further that these products of the human brain, like religious ideas, have 'a life of their own'—a life explored in depth by Walter Benjamin in his study of Baudelaire. Both Marx and Benjamin are relevant to Adorno's use of the term here. For a discusssion of the concept, see Gillian Rose, *The Melancholy Science: An Introduction to the Thought of Theodor W. Adorno*, Macmillan 1978, pp. 30–1, 40–2, 47. *Translator's note.*

primacy of harmonic and instrumental sound in his music. The great phantasmagorias that recur again and again occupy a central position in his work, one where all movement has its origins. They are all defined in terms of the medium of sound: 'Wondrously, from afar, the dulcet tones resound', as it is put in the *Venusberg* scene in *Tannhäuser*, the phantasmagoria par excellence. Until its dissolution with Schreker, the Neo-German school remained loyal to the idea of 'distant sound', as the source of acoustic delusion; in it music pauses and is made spatial, the near and the far are deceptively merged, like the comforting Fata Morgana that brings the mirage of cities and caravans within reach and makes social models appear magically rooted in nature. The phantasmagorical nature of the *Venusberg* music can be analysed technically. Its characteristic sound is created by the device of diminution. A diminished *forte* predominates, the image of loudness from afar. It is executed by light wood winds. Chief among them is the piccolo flute, the most archaic of all orchestral instruments and one almost entirely unaffected by advances in instrumental technique. It is a musical fairyland, not unlike the one that the young Mendelssohn had created and which the older Wagner still cherished. The Venusberg appears to Tannhäuser diminished in size. It is reminiscent of the distorting mirror effects of the Tanagra theatre that can still be found in fairgrounds and suburban cabarets. Tannhäuser mirrors the bacchanal from the remoteness of heathen prehistory on the dream stage of his own body. The bass instruments that mark the harmonic progression and hence the temporal character of music are lacking; its miniature form stamps this music with the imprint of an age now irredeemably lost. But when, in the *Venusberg* part of the overture, the cellos and the basses enter at B, with the *ritardando*, what they mark is the moment when the dreamer becomes conscious of his own body and stretches in his sleep. The technique of diminishing the sound by eliminating the bass also confers the quality of phantasmagoria on a passage in *Lohengrin*, one which, less obviously than in *Tannhäuser*, determines the character of the whole work. It is Elsa's vision in which she conjures up the knight and thus launches the entire action. Her description of the knight resembles the picture of Oberon: the inward Lohengrin is a tiny fairy prince.

Arrayed in shining armour a knight was approaching,
more virtuous and pure than any I had yet seen,
a golden horn at his hip and leaning on his sword.
Thus was this worthy knight sent to me from heaven. (Act I, sc. 2)

Such bass notes as occur are given once more to ethereal
instruments such as the bass clarinets or the harp. The sound of the
bass clarinets, which is particularly transparent, never descends
below the E flat below the middle C. The horn referred to in the
text is conveyed on a diminished scale in the music by a trumpet in
pianissimo. The entrance of the basses at the words 'with courteous
bearing' is equivalent to the one in the *Tannhäuser* passage and
serves to relate the music, which had seemed to be floating
spellbound in the air, to the body of the dreaming woman.

'He gave me consolation'—a consolation that derives from the
Fata Morgana. The consoling phantasmagoria is that of the Grail
itself, and just as Elsa's vision contains motivs related to the Grail
theme, so, too, the *Lohengrin* prelude, which is an allegorical
representation of the Grail, contains the same technical features as
Elsa's vision. Even the caesura in the harmonic progression at the
beginning of the *Lohengrin* prelude becomes meaningful in terms
of phantasmagoria. The absence of any real harmonic progression
becomes the phantasmagorical emblem for time standing still.
Tannhäuser says in the *Venusberg*:

> The time I dwell here with thee, by days I cannot measure,
> seasons pass me, how, I scarcely know,
> —the radiant sun I see no longer,
> strange hath become the heaven's starry splendour—
> the sweet verdure of spring, the gentle token
> of earth's renewing life.[2]

The standing-still of time and the complete occultation of nature
by means of phantasmagoria are thus brought together in the
memory of a pristine age where time is guaranteed only by the
stars. Time is the all-important element of production that
phantasmagoria, the mirage of eternity, obscures. While days and

---

[2] Act I, sc. 2

months run into each other and vanish as in a moment, phantasmagoria makes up for this by representing the moment as that which endures. This is the case with *The Flying Dutchman*. The opera was originally conceived as a One-Acter with its roots in Senta's ballad. Even as a complete work it could be reduced to the moment when the Dutchman steps beneath—one could almost say, steps out from—his picture, as Senta, who has conjured him up as Elsa had conjured up the knight, stands gazing into his eyes. The entire opera is nothing more than the attempt to unfold this moment in time and, in its feebler passages, particularly in the case of a dramatic prop like Erik, the traces of the effort this entailed are all too obvious. The later works have greater success in articulating the phantasmagoria as drama without falsifying it. In *Parsifal* the phantasmagoria is transferred into the realm of the sacred which, for all that, retains elements of magical enchantment. On the way to the Grail the following conversation takes place:

GURNEMANZ: Methinks I knew you aright:
No way leads through the land to it,' [—to the Grail]
'And no one could find it,
Save the Grail lead him there.
PARSIFAL: I hardly move,
Yet far I seem to have come.
GURNEMANZ: You see, my son, time ||
changes here to space.[3] ||

The characters cast off their empirical being in time as soon as the ethereal kingdom of essences is entered. If, in his last years, Wagner flirted with the idea of metempsychosis, there is scant need to attribute this to the stimulus provided by Schopenhauer's Buddhist sympathies. Phantasmagoria had already enabled the pagan goddess Venus to migrate into the Christian era; she is reborn there just like Kundry, whom Klingsor conjures up as he lies sleeping in the blue light:

Herodias you were—and what besides?
Gundryggia there, Kundry here! (Act II)

[3] Act I, sc. 1.

Even the *Ring* gives evidence of a like intention when Brünnhilde's love for Siegfried turns out to be primordial in nature, referring to his image rather than his empirical self:

> I fed your tender being
> Before you were begotten;
> Even before you were born
> My shield protected you:
> So long have I loved you Siegfried! (*Siegfried*, Act III, sc. 3)

The only reason why Wagner's characters can function as universal symbols is that they dissolve in the phantasmagoria like mist.

Brünnhilde too is detached from time, sleeping like Kundry, in the abruptly invoked phantasmagoria of the magic fire—the dominant phantasmagoria of the *Ring* and the one from which, musically, the image of the twilight of the Gods is ultimately derived. While the manner of its production is completely concealed in its string sections, harmonically, its progression is most ingeniously that of a state of rest. Not only do the constant harmonic changes produce new progressions; at the same time, systematic modulation through the changing surfaces of the different keys makes the music dance round the basic harmonies which remain constant at any given moment, like a fire that perpetually flickers without ever moving from the spot. As a metaphor for fire, the final 60 bars of *The Valkyrie* provide crucial insight into the nature of phantasmagoria. Wagner's successors have termed them magic, but this is really valid only in the inauthentic sense of theatrical illusion. They belong with the series of dramas whose elements the *Dutchman* first illustrates, and which continues with the storm in the ride of the Valkyries, where the allegory ceases to be mere atmospheric background and actually enters into the action. The final stage is reached in the Good Friday music in *Parsifal* where no more is said of the miracle than that 'forest and meadow glisten in the morning light'. As a natural phenomenon the light touches them, imbuing them with the expression of reconciliation proper to the dew and tear. But Wagner's phantasmagorias are normally worlds removed from such unassuming appearances. One is tempted to derive them from the magic formula of earlier Romantic music; from Mendelssohn's *Midsummer Night's Dream* music as well as the spirit passages in *Euryanthe*, the musical visions of *Oberon*, and especially, the chthonic second themes in Schubert. And the heritage of that Romanticism is undeniably present in the dualism of waking and dreaming music that governs the overture to *Tannhäuser*, to name but one example, where the Pilgrims' procession fades away only to conjure up the *Venusberg*, as if in a dream.

But the specific quality of the Wagnerian phantasmagoria can only be discovered once it parts company with the magic music of Romanticism. Paul Bekker has made the extremely important observation that what separates Wagner from earlier Romanticism is that his music no longer contains 'real spirits'. 'By locating the miraculous in the human soul, he endows it with truth in the artistic sense and intensifies the world of saga and fairy-tale into the illusion of the absolute reality of the unreal.'[4] If we leave aside the dubious notion of 'truth in the artistic sense' and discard the category of interiorization as irrevelant to Wagner, the concept of illusion as the absolute reality of the unreal grows in importance. It sums up the unromantic side of the phantasmagoria: phantasmagoria as the point at which aesthetic appearance becomes a function of the character of the commodity. As a commodity it purveys illusions. The absolute reality of the unreal is nothing but the reality of a phenomenon that not only strives unceasingly to spirit away its own origins in human labour, but also, inseparably from this process and in thrall to exchange value, assiduously emphasizes its use value, stressing that this is its authentic reality, that it is 'no imitation'—and all this in order to further the cause of exchange value. In Wagner's day the consumer goods on display turned their phenomenal side seductively towards the mass of customers while diverting attention from their merely phenomenal character, from the fact that they were beyond reach. Similarly, in the phantasmagoria, Wagner's operas tend to become commodities. Their tableaux assume the character of wares on display. As it flares up into a vast magic conflagration, the little Romantic flame of *Hans*

---

4 Bekker, p. 128.

Heiling[5] is transformed into the prototype of future illuminated advertisements. Wotan's slogan—

> Whoever fears the tip of my spear
> Shall never pass through the fire! (*Valkyrie*, Act III, sc. 3)

—could easily be supplemented by copy in praise of a piece of equipment that would enable the cautious but resolute buyer to pass through the fire notwithstanding. The Wagnerian phantasmagorias are among the earliest 'wonders of technology' to gain admittance to great art, and Wotan is not just the allegory of the self-denying will to live, but also the reliable exponent of a natural world that has been perfectly reproduced and wholly mastered. The phantasmagorical style immortalizes the moment between the death of Romanticism and the birth of realism. Its miracles have become as impenetrable as the daily reality of a reified society and hence enter into the inheritance of the magic powers that the Romantics had assigned to the transcendental sphere. But in their magic they simultaneously function as commodities that satisfy the needs of the culture market. The *Venusberg*, which was perfected at the climax of *Tristan* and was recalled yet again as a pale echo in the flower-girl scene in *Parsifal*, arose out of the ordinary theatrical requirements of the ballet. These are the only scenes in which Wagner's work is directly affected by the conditions of commodity production; but it is precisely these scenes in which the music takes the greatest care to disguise its production in a passive, visionary presence. Where the dream is at its most exalted, the commodity is closest to hand. The phantasmagoria tends towards dream not merely as the deluded wish-fulfilment of would-be buyers, but chiefly to conceal the labour that has gone into making it. It mirrors subjectivity by confronting the subject with the product of its own labour, but in such a way that the labour that has gone into it is no longer identifiable. The dreamer encounters his own image impotently, as if it were a miracle, and is held fast in the inexorable circle of his own labour, as if it would last for ever.

[5] An opera by Marschner to a libretto by Devrient that was originally written for Mendelssohn. Hans Heiling was a gnome king who unsuccessfully courts a human girl. *Translator's note.*

The object that he has forgotten he has made is dangled magically before his eyes, as if it were an absolutely objective manifestation.

Governed by the logic of dreams, the phantasmagoria succumbs to its own particular dialectic. This is most fully developed in *Tannhäuser*. With his very first words the enchantment is seen to be a dream:

Too much, too much! Oh that I now might waken! (Act I, sc. 2)

The mainspring of the action is encapsulated in that 'Too much!'. Like the victims of oppression, Tannhäuser is not equal to his own demands for pleasure. Nothing less than the ideal of freedom itself is used to justify his turning towards asceticism:

> And yet for earth, for earth I'm yearning,
> In thy soft chains with shame I'm burning,
> 'Tis freedom I must win or die,
> For freedom I can all defy. (Ibid.)

This is Tannhäuser's reply to Venus's Feuerbachian promise of bliss:

> Thou shalt no more love's timid victim be
> Rejoice with love's goddess in harmony! (Ibid.)

His wish is to take the image of pleasure away from the *Venusberg* and return with it to earth: his parting from Venus is one of the authentic political moments in Wagner's works. But, significantly, it becomes ambiguous. For fidelity to Venus is a commitment not to pleasure, but only to the phantasmagoria of pleasure. As he takes his leave, he vows:

> To strife and glory, forth I go
> Come life or death, come joy or woe! (Ibid.)

But, as it turns out, he keeps his other promise better:

> While I have life my harp shall praise but thee alone. (Ibid.)

His betrayal is not that he returns to the knights, but that with his mind still fixed on his dream, he naively sings them the hymn in praise of Venus—the same hymn that exposes him for a second time to the reproaches of the world from which he had once before fled into the phantasmagoria. But his outburst is a pretence: it leads from the *Venusberg* to the song contest, from dream to song, and the only surviving trace of what had originally led him to rebel is the beautiful song of the shepherd who celebrates the productivity of nature herself, beyond dream and captivity, as the work of the same power that had seemed mere slavery to the enchanted Tannhäuser. Venus is vindicated not by Tannhäuser's treacherous praise, but by the words,

> Dame Holda stepp'd from the mountain's heart . . . (Act I, sc. 3)

The socially determined experience of pleasure as unfreedom transforms libido into sickness, and so we see how, with the cry of 'Too much!', Tannhäuser becomes conscious of his own enjoyment as a weakness while he is still in the kingdom of Venus. The experience of pleasure as sickness permeates Wagner's entire oeuvre. Those who refuse to resign themselves—Tannhäuser, Tristan, Amfortas—are all 'sick'. In the story of Tannhäuser's pilgrimage to Rome we hear, to the accompaniment of music of the greatest power, music whose force is surpassed in Wagner only in Tristan's curse:

> Then I drew near,—my glances earthward bending,
> I made my plaint, despair my bosom rending;
> I told what mad desires my soul had darken'd,
> What longing by no atonement yet appeas'd. (Act III, sc. 3)

Sickness and desire become confounded in a point of view that imagines that the forces of life can only be maintained by the suppression of life. In the Wagnerian theatre desire sinks to the level of caricature: to that image of bloated pallor that seems the perfect complement to the castrati-like physique of the tenors. In a regression familiar from the process of bourgeois education and known to psychoanalysis as 'syphilophobia' (sex and sexual disease become identical. It is no accident that one of Wagner's objections to vivisection was that the knowledge gleaned from such experimentation might lead to the curing of diseases that had been contracted through 'vice'. The conversion of pleasure into sickness is the denunciatory task of phantasmagoria. If two of the Wagnerian phantasmagorias, the *Venusberg* and Klingsor's enchanted garden, are reminiscent of dreamland brothels, these are simultaneously calumniated as places that no one can leave unscathed. And without a doubt all of Wagner's profound ingenuity was required to reconcile us to the flower girls[6] when he had condemned them from the outset as 'worthless sirens'.[7] It has been observed that the flutes that are heard throughout the *Venusberg* seldom recur as solo instruments in Wagner's later work. They too are victims of the denigration of pleasure in the phantasmagoria, the same pleasure that it was their function to represent. Nietzsche was well aware of this: 'What do I suffer from when I suffer from the fate of music? From the fact that music has been stripped of its ability to transfigure and affirm the world, that it is decadent music and no longer the flute of Dionysus.'[8] The Wagnerian flute is that of the Pied Piper of Hamelin; but as such it is instantly tabooed.

With the anathematizing of the very pleasure it puts on display, the phantasmagoria is infected from the outset with the seeds of its own destruction. Inside the illusion dwells disillusionment. Within Wagner's work this phenomenon has its own highly recondite model: that of *Don Quixote*, a book that Wagner held in particular esteem. The phantasmagoria of *The Mastersingers*, in Act II, puts its hero into the role of the man who fights against windmills. Walther Stolzing who wishes to re-establish the old feudal immediacy, as opposed to the bourgeois division of labour enshrined in the guilds, becomes a potential figure of comedy in the face of a bourgeois reality in which the feudal world is transformed into myth before his very eyes. At the call of the night-watchman 'he claps his hand to his sword and stares wildly before him', while the bourgeois Eva instructs him:

[6] See *Parsifal*, Act II.
[7] Hildebrandt, p. 377.
[8] Quoted by Hildebrandt, p. 440.

> Beloved, spare your anger!
> It was only the nightwatchman's horn. (Act II, sc. 5)

The Beckmesser scene and the scene of the brawl are enacted within the confines of ordinary reality and only a Don Quixote like Walther could experience them as uncanny or nightmarish. However, the bourgeois world generates elements from within itself that objectively assume the very quality of illusion that is created subjectively in the dreamworld of Romantic protest. A pre-established harmony is created between the monad that seeks refuge from the guild-masters in the vanished world of castle, court and troubadour song, and the bourgeois world of the masters themselves which adopts the mask of a bygone age because it does not feel at home in the present. Since the guilds can no longer understand each other's point of view and so accuse each other of the dishonesty that characterizes them all, there is a momentary flare-up of prehistoric anarchy in the street brawl, which is merely a poor substitute for political action; and similarly in the song contest on the Wartburg which *The Mastersingers* had set out to parody. Bourgeois innovation and archaic regression meet in the phantasmagoria, so that objectively the knight's dream is vindicated. The spooky nature of the phantasmagoria in Act III is confirmed by Sachs, and thereby the ultimate ground of the dream is reached:

> A goblin must have helped!
> A glow-worm could not find its mate;
> It set the trouble in motion. (Act III, sc. 1)

The dream of Act II is interpreted by Sachs as the product of repression; but glow-worms are Nature's own Chinese lanterns: phantasmagoria comes into being when, under the constraints of its own limitations, modernity's latest products come close to the archaic. Every step forwards is at the same time a step into the remote past. As bourgeois society advances it finds that it needs its own camouflage of illusion simply in order to subsist. For only when so disguised does it venture to look the new in the face. That formula, 'it sounded so old, and yet was so new', is the cypher of a social conjuncture. When the generous Pogner, who said himself that God had made him a wealthy man, wants to break out of the narrow confines of the petty bourgeoisie and prove that he is not avaracious and small-minded, the only means at his disposal is the farce of the mythic song contest. The impoverished imaginative world of the bourgeois produces an image of itself in the phantasmagoric, and Wagner's work serves this image as it serves the bourgeois. As the blueprint of a pristine bourgeois world *The Mastersingers* is therefore his central work: 'Thus in the completion and production of *The Mastersingers*, which I at first desired in Nuremberg, I was governed by the idea of offering the German public an image of its own true nature, so botched for it before; and cherished the hope of winning from the nobler, stouter class of German burghers a hearty salutation in return.'[9] However, this salutation is the expression of gratitude both for the dream and for its destruction, and the asceticism which Wagner takes upon himself for the sake of freedom finally turns against freedom. By appealing to the Virgin Mary he destroys the image of beauty that promises more than an ideal belonging to the past, and when the sacred spear hovers phantasmagorically above Parsifal's head, he incorporates it in a curse:

> Let it destroy this fraudulent luxury
> In rack and ruin! (Act II)

It is the curse of the rebel who in his youth had stormed the unforgotten brothels.

---

[9] *Richard Wagner's Prose Works*, Vol. 6, p. 114.

7

Music Drama

The celebration of a phantasmagoric world by no means exhausts Wagner's aesthetic repertoire. Both the phantasmagoria and the rhythm of its dissolution have to be articulated in a large-scale epic work of art. The overarching structure that results is the *Gesamtkunstwerk*—or, as Wagner preferred to call it, the 'drama of the future'—in which poetry, music and theatre were united. Even though his intention was to obliterate the frontiers separating the individual arts in the name of an all-pervasive infinity and even though the experience of synaesthesia is one of the corner-stones of Romanticism, the *Gesamtkunstwerk* is actually unrelated to the Romantic theories of fifty years earlier. For in seeking an aesthetic interchangeability, and by striving for an artifice so perfect that it conceals all the sutures in the final artefact and even blurs the difference between it and nature itself, it presupposes the same radical alienation from anything natural that its attempt to establish itself as a unified 'second nature' sets out to obscure. Astonishingly enough, Wagner himself become aware of the element of concealment implicit in the phantasmagoria, in the course of his discussion of the unified nature of the *Gesamtkunstwerk*. And he did so, moreover, at the precise point where he sets out to characterize the 'poetic aim' from which the work springs: 'Such an expression must contain the poet's aim in each of its separate moments, albeit in each of them concealing that aim from the feeling—to wit, by realizing it. Even to Word-Tone-speech this entire cloaking of the poetic aim would be impossible, were it not that a second, a concurrent organ of Tone-speech could be allied therewith; so that wherever Word-Tone-speech—as the directest harbourer of the poet's aim, and for the sake of keeping it in touch with the moods of ordinary life—is obliged to so thin down its own expression, that it can only clothe that aim with an almost diaphanous veil of tone, there this second organ is able to maintain an even balance of the one emotional expression.'[1]

The concealment of the process of poetic production for the sake of its aim, that is to say, its rationale, as well as the constitutive relationship to 'ordinary life'[2] which Opera and Drama never tires of recalling, are thereby inserted by Wagner himself into the configuration defining the phantasmagoria. The 'second speech-organ', then, is none other than the orchestra, the medium of Wagner's phantasmagoria. The emancipation of colour achieved by the orchestra intensifies the element of illusion by transferring the emphasis from the essence, the musical event in itself, to the apperance, the sound. Innovations, such as the creation of musical spaces composed of orchestral colour, can be achieved only at the expense of articulation in time, and for the benefit of the dazzling present. Ultimately it is this illusory present that derives greatest advantage from the undermining of the constructivist elements in Wagner's composition. With the 'concealment of the poetic aim', the Gesamtkunstwerk strives towards the ideal of the absolute phenomenon which the phantasmagoria dangles so tantalizingly before it: 'We thus designate the most perfect unity of artistic form as that in which a widest conjuncture of the phenomena of human life—as content—can impart itself to the feeling in so completely intelligible an expression that in all its moments this content shall completely stir, and also completely satisfy, the feeling. The content, then, has to be one that is ever present in the expression, and therefore the expression one that ever presents the content in its fullest compass; for whereas the absent can be grasped only by thought, only the present can be grasped by feeling.'[3]

Plausible as such a sentimental aesthetics of 'pure feeling' must have sounded to the ears of the nineteenth-century bourgeoisie, to whom it was self-evident long before Hermann Cohen gave it a name, it nevertheless remains true that it scarcely does justice to

[1] Richard Wagner's Prose Works, Vol. 2, pp. 344–45.
[2] Ibid., p. 338.
[3] Ibid., pp. 348–49.

music. Music can only be bodied forth in the present as a result of
the most intense effort of memory and anticipation. This effort is
the task of authentic thematic work, something evaded in
Wagner's case by the trick of using extra-musical mnemonics in
the form of motivs charged with allegorical meanings. The
innermost weakness of this aesthetic, of the theory as well as its
practice, lies in the fact that the mosaic of thing-like or piece-like
elements that cannot be wholly actualized proves too powerful to
be absorbed into the aesthetic whole. In consequence they are
instead denied and spirited away. The permanent process of
making-present is what music is supposed to achieve, by working
on poetry at the expense of musical time. The aim of this process is
to dissolve and revitalize the unyielding thing-like nature of
poetry, and with it the reflex of the world of commodities in art,
and so to transform it into the radiant manifestation of pure
subjective actuality. 'Science has laid bare to us the organism of
speech; but what she showed us was a defunct organism, which
only the poet's utmost want can bring to life again; and that by
healing up the wounds with which the anatomic scalpel has gashed
the body of speech and by breathing into it the breath that may
animate it with living motion. This breath, however, is—music.'[4]
Music is called upon to do nothing less than retract the historical
tendency of language, which is based on signification, and to
substitute expressiveness for it. Wagner is the first to insert the
uneven development of the arts, its very irrationality, into a
rationally planned framework—albeit, initially at least, only an
aesthetic one. As has been pointed out in a recent work on the
aesthetics of the cinema, 'the adaptation to the order of bourgeois
rationality and, ultimately, the age of advanced industry, which
was made by the eye when it accustomed itself to perceiving reality
as a reality of objects and hence basically of commodities, was not
an adaptation made simultaneously by the ear. Compared with
seeing, hearing is "archaic" and has lagged behind technology. It
could be said that to react with the unselfconscious ear rather than
with the nimble, appraising eye is somehow in contradiction to the
advanced-industrial era . . . The eye is always the organ of effort,

[4] Ibid., p. 265.

work, concentration; it apprehends something specific in an unambiguous way. The ear, in contrast, is unconcentrated and passive. Unlike the eye, it does not have to be opened. Compared to the eye it has something dozy and inert about it. But this doziness is overlaid with the taboo that society has placed on all laziness. Music has always been a stratagem for outwitting this taboo.'[5] Nowadays dozing is subject to psycho-technical control, but Wagner, by following the thrust and even the dire need of his own talent, was the first to discover the effects it might be made to yield. This was something that Nietzsche rightly suspected to be the case. The unconscious, which Wagner learned about from Schopenhauer, has already become ideology for him: the task of music is to warm up the alienated and reified relations of men and make them sound as if they were still human. This technological hostility to consciousness is the very foundation of the music drama. It combines the arts in order to produce an intoxicating brew. Wagner's language, a synthesis of idealism and lust, formulates it in a metaphor of sexual congress: 'The necessary bestowal, the seed that can only in the most ardent transports of love condense itself from his noblest forces—this procreative seed is the poetic aim, which brings to the glorious loving woman, Music, the stuff for bearing.'[6] Wagner's practice adhered enthusiastically to this metaphor. Not only do the music dramas culminate in ecstatic passages like Isolde's last song, the Siegfried-Brünnhilde scene at the end of *Siegfried* or Brünnhilde's lamentation in *Twilight of the Gods*—but also, because of the promiscuousness of its elements, the very form of the music drama is a permanent invitation to intoxication, as a form of 'oceanic regression'. The *Twilight of the Gods*, which conducts the listener, as it were interminably, on a great voyage, seems to flood the whole world with music, and even though it actually has little success in melting down the mass of material into lyric, it makes up for this by the way in which the hard, unyielding outlines are inundated by the waves. In the late Wagner it is not just the

[5] Adorno gave no source for this passage, in which he is in fact quoting himself. Cf. Adorno and Hanns Eisler, *Komposition für den Film*, Munich 1969, pp. 41, 43. *Note by the German editor.*

[6] *Richard Wagner's Prose Works*, Vol. 2, p. 236.

dividing lines between the different arts that become blurred; even the works seem to run into each other. The fact that he is an allegorist shows itself not least in the way in which everything can come to mean the same as everything else. Forms and symbols become intermingled until Sachs becomes Mark, the Grail becomes the Nibelungs hoard and Nibelungs become Wibelungs. The basic idea of the music drama is revealed not so much in the music, but rather by a sort of mental flight, by the jettisoning of everything unequivocal, and by the negation of everything with an individual stamp.

This basic idea is that of totality: the *Ring* attempts, without much ado, nothing less than the encapsulation of the world process as a whole. Wagner's impatience towards everything isolated, everything limited and existing simply for itself, towards all the things on which his phantasmagorical musical procedures feed, is a protest against the bourgeoisification of art that rests content with metaphors of dour self-preservation. The methods by which Wagner blurs all dividing lines, and the monumental scale of both his subjects and his works, are inseparable from his longing to create in the 'grand style', a longing already inherent in the masterful gesture of the conductor. The Wagnerian totality is the enemy of genre art. Like Baudelaire's, his reading of bourgeois high capitalism discerned an anti-bourgeois, heroic message in the destruction of *Biedermeier*. He detested the sacrifices that the last substantial social style imposed on art to enable its survival in the age of individualism, and had penetrated the laws governing the movement of society deeply enough to perceive the impotence of a principle of selection founded on obstinate ignorance of them. He rebels against a false sense of security and, blind to the possibility of any other, goes out in search of dangerous living. Like Nietzsche and subsequently Art Nouveau, which he anticipates in many respects, he would like single-handed to will an aesthetic totality into being, casting a magic spell and with defiant unconcern about the absence of the social conditions necessary for its survival.

It may well be the case that, alongside the concept of the technical work of art, Wagner's works mark the introduction of the 'will to style' [*Stilwille*]. He protests at the narrowness of an objective spirit whose social and aesthetic subject has shrunk to the dimensions of the private individual. His own starting-point, however, which is itself merely aesthetic, remains dependent on the listening habits of that individual, on what he is able to create on his own and on the transcendence he would like to be able to achieve in the name of society as a whole. For this reason the Wagnerian totality, the *Gesamtkunstwerk*, is doomed to failure. To disguise this is not the least of Wagner's tasks in running all the different elements into each other. The greater the failure of the music drama as style, the more it strives for stylization. The whole no longer achieves unity, because its expressive elements are made to harmonize with each other according to a pre-arranged design, possibly of a conventional nature. Instead, the different arts which are now alienated from each other and cannot be reconciled by any meaning, are yoked together 'at the arbitrary fiat of the isolated artist. The formal premisses of an internal logic are replaced by a seamless external principle in which disparate procedures are simply aggregated in such a way as to make them appear collectively binding. Unity of style is usurped by features of the private individual and, moreover, of the onlooker as Wagner imagines him. The style becomes the sum of all the stimuli registered by the totality of his senses. The universe of perceptions at his disposal offers itself as a coherent totality of meaning, as the fullness of life: hence the fictive nature of the Wagnerian style. For in the contingent experience of individual bourgeois existence the separate senses do not unite to create a totality, a unified and guaranteed world of essences. It is questionable, indeed, whether such a unity of sense experience has ever existed, dependent on it as Wagner's disillusioned mind may be. On the contrary, the senses, which all have a different history, end up poles apart from each other, as a consequence of the growing reification of reality as well as of the division of labour. For this not only separates men from each other but also divides each man with himself. It is for this reason that the music drama proves unable to assign meaningful functions to the different arts. Its form, therefore, is that of a spurious identity. Music, scene and words are integrated only in the sense that the author—the freakishness of his position is well suggested by the term 'poet-composer'—treats them as if they all converged on the same goal. But he only achieves this by doing

them violence and hence distorting the whole, which ends up in
tautology, as permanent over-determination. The music repeats
what the words have already said and the more it pushes itself to
the fore the more superfluous it becomes, when measured against
the meaning it is supposed to express. And this in turn affects the
integrity of the music. The very attempt to adapt the arts to each
other disrupts the unity of compositional structure. The *Sprech-
gesang* was the means devised by Wagner to act as the guarantor of
that unity. The idea was that a quasi-natural intonation would
harmonize music and language without doing violence to either.
But this had the effect that the singing voice, the as it were palpable
bearer of the musical action, the universal object of attention at the
opera, is separated by force from the actual musical content. Apart
from the few passages in which the dominance of the musical form
can be conceded, the singing voice is detached from the life of
music and its logic: to sing a motiv would conflict with the
requirement of a natural intonation and would depart from the
normal inflection of speech. In Wagner's music the most vital
elements, song and the orchestra, necessarily diverge. Song, the
most immediate of the two, ceases to be involved in the most
essential part, the thematic texture, except in the abstract and non-
committal sense that the singing voice follows the orchestral
harmonies. In order to bring about the synthesis of all the arts, the
internal consistency of the most crucial element, the music, is
set aside.

The (pseudo-adaptation of music to language) has progressed
inexorably ever since the emergence of the *stile rappresentativo*, to
which music owes so much of its liberation. But it reveals its
negative side the moment it becomes parasitical upon language
and slavishly follows the curve of the linguistic flow. At the same
time the music becomes a commentary on the stage, since the
author takes up an attitude and violates the very ideal of immanent
form in the name of which the music drama was originally
conceived. This explains the intermittent, dragging effect so
suggestive of the film. The words, uttered with one eye fixed on
the music, as it were, are constantly overdoing things; Wagner's
theatricality is inseparable from the *terminus ad quem* of the
poetry which always has to move in extremes in order to keep pace

with the music. Whereas for its part, the music, because of its extra, interpretative function, finds itself drained of all the energies that make it a language remote from meaning, pure sound, and so contrast it with human sign-language, a contrast by virtue of which its full humanity is made possible. And, finally, the stage is compelled to go along with what is happening in the orchestra. The infantile actions of the singers—the opera often seems like a museum of long-forgotten gestures—are caused by their adaption to the flow of the music. They resemble the music, but falsely; they become caricatures, because each set of gestures effectively mimics those of the conductor. The closer and the more indiscreetly the different arts are brought into proximity, and the more the music drama approaches their fundamental indifference to each other, the more they prove mutually disruptive. The older opera, which Wagner accused of lacking aesthetic unity because it had failed to integrate the different arts, was superior to him at least in one respect: it sought unity not in the assimilation of one art to the other, but in complying with the laws governing each separate realm. Mozartian unity was that of configuration, not identification. In Wagner, however, the radical process of integration, which assiduously draws attention to itself, is already no more than a cover for the underlying fragmentation. The cosmos of what can be perceived, which in his work is supposed to represent an essence—because the only thing in which the isolated individual can put his trust is the totality of what his senses can grasp with certainty—this cosmos has no reality. What holds it together is nothing more than the chance existence of each individual. But as a merely contingent being that usurps the status of a necessary existence, the *Gesamtkunstwerk* must inevitably fail. For in advanced bourgeois civilization every organ of sense apprehends, as it were, a different world, if not indeed a different time, and so the style of the music drama cannot entrust itself to any single sense, but must instead transform one into the other in order thereby to bring about something of the harmony that they lack. But it will find this impossible as long as the different organs are referred to the judgment of consciousness. It can only work as long as the sense organs resist any authority that distinguishes between them and instead regress to a sort of archaic mélange. In the *Gesamtkunstwerk*, intoxication, ecstasy, is an inescapable principle of style; a moment of reflection would suffice to shatter its illusion of ideal unity.

However, the emotional thrust of the *Gesamtkunstwerk* is directed not just against the conciliatory genre music of *Biedermeier*, but also against the art forms of Wagner's own industrial age, during which the genre elements of *Biedermeier* were converted into consumer articles. To the dissatisfied aesthete in his flight from banality, gods, heroes and a dramatic action encompassing the universe hold out the promise of salvation. Earlier Romanticism had not stood in need of quite such grandiose images, because it did not have to face the constant threat of commoditization which ultimately contaminates even Wagner's own heroic models. In his efforts to achieve a totality of the senses he begins by issuing a categorical call for the emancipation of the ear, which is, as he says, 'no child'.[7] In doing this he is tilting against the attitude that would 'degrade the sense of hearing to a servile porter for its bales of industrial goods'.[8] However, the idea of totality that inspires the music drama cannot tolerate a mere antithesis to 'ordinary life'. It knows that there are weighty reasons why it has to coopt that existence at the same time as the artist strives to escape from the everyday world for reasons no less cogent. That is to say, the entanglement in the banal is as total as the flight from it. In *Tristan* that world of banality is by no means confined to the 'day' that the 'action' would like to exchange for the kingdom of the night. The action culminates in the decision to die. Death will recall to the ultimate ground of being the finite individuals whose infinite yearnings are doomed to suffer such torments in the finite world. However, this decision, which is meant to 'redeem' the individual not just from the day, but from individuation itself, is clothed in an image that is itself banal. For the musical image-world posited as the metaphysical antithesis of the isolated monad is derived from the very society it negates. What presents itself as a corrective to mere individualism, turns out to be the approved musical language, and the individual who chooses the night involuntarily sells himself to the existing order.

[7] Ibid., p. 271.
[8] Ibid., p. 270

No unprejudiced person who listens to the rapturous 'motiv of the resolve to die' in *Tristan* for the first time, will be able to escape the impression of frivolous gaiety. From the perspective of the individual, essence, the universal, can only be evoked as a bad universal. In order to vindicate death from outside the individuality that it sets out to annihilate, the metaphysico-psychological scheme of *Tristan* is compelled to equate death with pleasure. But as a positive fact, however, the image of pleasure lapses into the everyday. It becomes the élan of the individual who wills it thus, who in that very act of will participates in life, thereby proclaiming his complicity with it. And with this the Wagnerian metaphysics of death pays its tribute to the unattainability of joy which ever since Beethoven has remained valid for all great music. There is an inexorable logic in the way the tragic decision turns into the gesture 'What price the world?', and the rapturous *Liebestod* into a soloist's hit song. The monad-like individual, to whom the composer remains loyal and from whose perspective he composes, is not the absolute antithesis of society: the nature of his being follows from society's own principles. The social destiny of loneliness, a ruthless impulse to express oneself and an element of vulgar self-assertiveness and self-praise are only too compatible. Even in Wagner's lifetime, and in flagrant contradiction to his programme, star numbers like the Fire Music and Wotan's farewell, the Ride of the Valkyries, the *Liebestod* and the Good Friday music had been torn out of their context, re-arranged and become popular. This fact is not irrelevant to the music dramas, which had cleverly calculated the place of these passages within the economy of the whole. The disintegration into fragments sheds light on the fragmentariness of the whole.

The cause of this fragmentation lies in the conflict between romantic and positivistic elements. The conception of an inwardly coherent self-unfolding totality, of the idea embodied in sensuous perception, is a late flower of the great metaphysical systems. The main thrust of these systems had been broken by Feuerbach, with whose works Wagner was acquainted, but it had found refuge in the realm of aesthetic form. Wagner may be believed when he says that when he finally read Schopenhauer, he was not 'influenced' by him in the usual sense, but merely felt himself confirmed. At all events, the shift from metaphysics into aesthetics is prepared in Book III of *The World as Will and Idea*. In Schopenhauer's case it is conditioned by the positivism that declares itself so clearly in his determination to deny 'meaning' to the realm of nature, which is left at the mercy of the blind Will. And similarly in Wagner the metaphysics implicit in his procedure is intimately related to the disenchantment of the world. The totality of the music drama is an aggregate of all the reactions of the sense organs and this aggregate is founded not only on the absence of a valid style, but even more on the dissolution of metaphysics. The aim of the *Gesamtkunstwerk* is not so much to express such a metaphysics as to produce it. A wholly profane outlook aspires to give birth to a sacred sphere from within itself; in this respect *Parsifal* merely makes conscious the tendency of the entire oeuvre. The deceptive character of the *Gesamtkunstwerk* stems from this fact. The work of art no longer conforms to the Hegelian definition that art is the sensuous manifestation of the idea. Instead, the sensuous is so arranged as to appear to be in control of the idea. This is the true basis of the allegorical element in Wagner: the conjuring up of essences beyond recall. The technological intoxication is generated from the fear of a sobriety that is all too close at hand. Thus we see that the evolution of the opera, and in particular the emergence of the autonomous sovereignty of the artist, is intertwined with the origins of the culture industry. Nietzsche, in his youthful enthusiasm, failed to recognize the artwork of the future in which we witness the birth of film out of the spirit of music. For this nexus there is an early piece of authentic evidence from Wagner's immediate circle. On 23 March 1890, that is to say, long before the invention of the cinema, Chamberlain wrote to Cosima about Liszt's *Dante* symphony, which can stand here for a whole tendency: 'Perform this symphony in a darkened room with a sunken orchestra and show pictures moving past in the background—and you will see how all the Levis and all the cold neighbours of today, whose unfeeling natures give such pain to a poor heart, will all fall into ecstasy.'[9] Few documents could

---

[9] *Cosima Wagner und Houston Stewart Chamberlain im Briefwechsel 1888 bis 1908*, ed. P. Pretzsch, Leipzig 1934, p. 146.

demonstrate more tellingly how inaccurate it is to assert that mass culture was imposed on art from outside. The truth is, it was thanks to its own emancipation that art was transformed into its opposite.

The flawed nature of the whole conception of music drama is nowhere more evident than where it comes closest to its own foundations: in the concealment of the process of production, in Wagner's hostility towards the division of labour on which it is agreed that the culture industry is based. In theory and in the ideology of his works, he rejected the division of labour in terms that recall National Socialist phrases about the subordination of private interests to the public good. In his anti-Semitic caricatures of Beckmesser and Mime, Wagner, the expert in orchestral and theatrical effects, has portrayed them as experts. What is supposed to be funny about them is that they have become so specialized that they are no longer capable of carrying out the tasks in which they have specialized. Beckmesser, the guild marker, can neither understand the prize song, nor, since his head is stuffed full of the rules of composition, can he produce one himself that manages even to be coherent. For his part, Mime, the smith, is 'too wise' to make the only sword he might need. In these two figures, Wagner pours scorn on reflective reason. As contrasting ideals, he sets up Walther and Siegfried, who stand for an undivided primordial world. This world is to be irrational, like the role of music in the *Gesamtkunstwerk* according to Wagner's programme. Walther refers to Nature as the teacher from whom he has picked up what he knows, and also to Walther von der Vogelweide—in whose poems, incidentally, as in those of his age, there is an almost total absence of what has been known, ever since the industrial revolution, as nature poetry. Wagner's idealism was such that he did not scruple to take enormous liberties with the facts whose aura he was so eager to enlist in the service of the *Gesamtkunstwerk*. However, even though he plays off the mythical unity of poet, singer and mime against the division of labour, and acts as if the *Gesamtkunstwerk* were capable of achieving that unity itself, the division of labour is in fact intensified rather than abolished by his techniques. The text of *The Mastersingers* is no less aware of contradiction than is Hegel in his call for objectivation. At the end, Walther the 'singer' bows down to Sachs the 'master' and learns not to 'despise' the specialized guilds. But we must note that this reconciliation of the feudal and bourgeois orders amounts to a complicity with the self-same reified world of which the Junker had rightly been afraid. Despite all this, however, there is little about Wagner that is more progressive than his paradoxical efforts to discover a rational way of overcoming conditions brought forth by a misguided use of reason. Many of Wagner's culture-loving and civilization-hating opponents, Hildebrandt among them, criticize him for having adopted without reservation the technical achievements of the nineteenth century, despite his alleged 'struggle' against them. They enumerate the sins of the Bayreuth 'stage mechanic', and would undoubtedly come to even more disconcerting conclusions if they could read a score. Wagner's intention of integrating the individual arts into the *Gesamt-kunstwerk* ends up by achieving a division of labour unprecedented in the history of music.

> The wound is healed only by the spear
> that caused it. (*Parsifal*, Act III)

—this might be the motto for Wagner's mode of composition. And it is precisely the religious *Parsifal* that makes use of the film-like technique of scene-transformation that marks the climax of this dialectic: the magic work of art dreams its complete antithesis, the mechanical work of art. The working methods of major composers have always contained elements of technical rational-izaton. We need only think of the cyphers and abbreviations in Beethoven's manuscripts. In his late works Wagner takes this practice to great lengths. Between the composition sketch and the full score a third form is inserted: the so-called orchestral sketch. Here the original pencilled draft is fully written out in ink—as it were, objectified. At the same time, the complete orchestration is added so that, while he was still at work on *Parsifal*, Wagner could say that the orchestral sketch would suffice to enable another person to produce the full score. The orchestral sketch—which is now called the short score—is established in parallel to the composition sketch; it follows it regularly at an interval of a few days. In this way the two procedures are clearly distinguished from each other, thus preventing the sound in Berlioz's sense from achieving independence. Control over it is reserved for the further process of composition. On the other hand, the short interval between the two stages makes it possible to retain a grasp of the orchestral colour that had been conceived in the original act of composition. This gives some indication of the ingenuity with which Wagner organized the division of labour. It encompasses all the layers of his composition and makes possible that interlocking of its elements, which closes all gaps and creates the impression of absolute cohesion and immediacy. The magical effect is inseparable from the same rational process of production that it attempts to exorcize.

Wagner's division of labour is that of an individual. This sets limits to it, which is perhaps why it has to be so strenuously denied. The objection to the music drama is not that it violates the allegedly absolute autonomy of the individual arts. This autonomy is in reality a fetish of the disciplines formed by the division of labour. When Wagner attacked it in the name of 'real', that is to say, a whole and free humanity, he was putting forward one of the demands of a true humanism. However, this demand turned into its opposite, into intoxication and delusion, instead of enlisting the rational control of the labour process in the cause of freedom. The explanation for this unexpected result is that the *Gesamtkunstwerk* is founded on the bourgeois 'individual' with his soul, whose origins and substance are rooted in the self-same alienation against which the *Gesamtkunstwerk* rebels. The latter is constituted not by the totality in whose name it resounds, but belongs, both in its premisses and its substance, to the individual. It makes strident claims to be the incarnation of the totality. According to Wagner's theory the emphatic role of the 'genius' falls to the poet, whose primacy he defends against his own true home, music, possibly because, as an expert, he mistrusts music. There can be no doubt that he was aware of the painful contradiction between individualism and the *Gesamtkunstwerk*, but he hoped that rapture would exorcize or transfigure it: 'Not to two, at the present time, can come the thought of jointly making possible the perfected drama; for, in parleying on this thought, the two must necessarily and candidly avow an impossibility of its realization in face of public life, and that avowal would nip their undertaking in the bud. Only the lonely man, in the thick of his endeavour, can transmute the bitterness of such a self-avowal into an intoxicating joy which drives him on with all the courage of a drunkard, to undertake the making possible of the impossible; for he, *alone*, is thrust forward by *two* artistic forces which he cannot withstand,—by forces which he willingly lets drive him to sacrifice himself.'[10] Even though these sentences contain much truth, they point not to the *Gesamt-kunstwerk*, but to its critical repudiation. Wagner's talk of self-sacrifice has less to do with the Flaubertian motif of self-torture than with his conviction that his cause is hopeless. The passage aims at more than the ecstatic surrender of individuation. What the individual abandons in the music drama is not himself, but the consistency of the work. As an isolated individual it is not actually within his power to abolish the division of labour to which he owes everything he achieves; all he can do is create the illusion for a time that he has done away with it. But by the same token, he is in no better position to transform himself into the specialist in every branch of the music drama that each art separately requires. The artist in his velvet jacket and beret who poses as a 'master', as the quintessential Artist, and the half-dilettantish poet who can never quite satisfy the demands of language and the stage—however contradictory they may seem, the two are really all of a piece. What the individual conceives of as an organic, living unity, stands revealed objectively as a mere agglomerate. The rationalization of technique, to which Wagner came closest in his treatment of musical material, failed everywhere else. A valid *Gesamtkunstwerk*, purged of its false identity, would have required a collective of specialist planners. Schoenberg, who, as a composer for the theatre, remained naively loyal to the Wagnerian aesthetics, once conceived the utopian idea of a 'composer's studio', in which each person would take up the work at the point where another has to give it up. However, collective labour is ruled out for Wagner, not simply by the social situation in the middle of the nineteenth century, but even more radically by the substance of his work, the metaphysics of yearning, rapture and redemption. This makes

[10] *Richard Wagner's Prose Works*, Vol. 2, p. 356.

impossible the only form in which the *Gesamtkunstwerk* could be organized collectively—an antithetical form. The principle of false identity does not allow the construction of a unity out of the contradictions between arts that are alienated from each other. In the history of bourgeois opera the justifying feature of music lay in its protest against the silent and senseless power of Fate—and in this respect the protest of Monteverdi's lamenting Ariadne is as effective as the *Fidelio* fanfare that reaches down into the dungeons. In Wagner, on the other hand, music has sold its right to protest. As an inexorable chain of cause and effect it remains as determinist as the philosophy he embraces and it runs its course as an unseeing doom. It is this that leads to the appearance, noted by his more responsible critics, both of pure form and of a profound hostility to form. The very seamlessness of the form of the music drama, the Wagnerian 'style' itself, is what is at fault. Music no longer possesses its decisive power: its ability to transcend imprisonment, in the context of an action. This is why it is reduced to overwhelming the listener with a passion and excitement that does not even pause for breath. The aesthetics of duplication is a substitute for protest, a mere amplification of subjective expression that is nullified by its very vehemence. But the individual arts whose rules are violated by the Wagnerian magic take their revenge by mocking the union and emphasizing their differences, which the work failed to fructify. Precisely because the music dramas refuse to loosen the texture for a single moment, we often find a greater surplus of prosaic subject matter over music than was ever the case in the traditional recitative, which never set out to transform the subject matter into music in the first place. And this surplus continues to reverberate musically in the contrived network of motivs that defies the Wagnerian call for 'immediacy'. Anyone who has not realized that the redemption motiv stands at the end of *The Twilight of the Gods* will find its music as incomprehensible as its poetry. This is the price that the music drama has to pay for its renunciation of a purely musical logic based on the structuring of internal time. It succumbs to rationalism for irrational reasons. By driving a wedge between reflection and immediacy, the music drama carries out a judgment on itself. It is analogous to that passed by Wagner's theory when it

describes poetry as the concern of reason and music as the concern
of feeling, and asserts that the task of the *Gesamtkunstwerk* is to
marry the two—a distinction that subjects the arts to a cliché in
order to harmonize them the more easily. The productive energy
of the music drama arises from the dream of the whole man: 'Just as
that man alone can display himself in full persuasiveness, who
announces himself to our ear and eye at once: so the message-
bearer of the inner man cannot completely convince our hearing,
until it addresses itself with equal persuasiveness to both "eye and
ear" of this hearing'. [11] But both the design and the practice of the
Gesamtkunstwerk stand condemned by Wagner's own critical
insight: 'No one can be better aware than myself, that the
realization of this drama depends on conditions which do not
lie within the will, nay, not even within the capability of the
single individual—were this capability infinitely greater than my
own—but only in community, and in a mutual co-operation
made possible thereby: whereas, at the present time, what prevails
is the direct antithesis of both these factors.

[11] Ibid., pp. 273–74.
[12] Ibid., p. 356n.

8

Myth

In order to formulate the dual position of the music drama in terms of stylistic history, we would have to say that it polemicizes both against the Romantic opera, which had been prettified and reduced to a genre, and against Grand Opera, the musical drama of intrigue. On the one hand, it bans the supernatural from the stage in the name of human significance, or reduces it to a metaphor of natural events. On the other hand, its claim to a universal humanism undermines the antithesis of magic, namely any factual historicity. The rapture of the phantasmagoria expels any concern with politics from opera. Even earlier than Wagner, Meyerbeer had already reduced political themes to mere spectacle, as in the technicolour films or biographies of the famous that the culture industry serves up to the market in our own day. There can be no doubt that the elimination of the political from Wagner's own work was, in part at least, the result of the disillusionment of the bourgeoisie after 1848, a disappointment outspokenly reflected in his correspondence. But it did not escape his contemporaries that even the historical subjects he did treat in his youth contained a reactionary potential that came to the surface only in his later works. According to Newman, A. B. Marx had this objection to *Lohengrin*: '*This* drama the drama of the future? . . . The Middle Ages a picture of our future, the outlived, the quite finished, the child of our hopes? Impossible! These sagas and fables . . . come to us now only as the echo of the long-dead times that are quite foreign to our spirit.'[1] It is conceivable that, with the anti-

[1] Newman, Vol. 1, p. 351.

Romanticism of Young Germany in mind,[2] Wagner was just as anxious to meet such objections as to distance himself from operatic fairy-tales. But it is no less certain that, for all the talk of 'ordinary life', he was unable to break away from a childhood stereotype of the poetic, and that he refused to jeopardize the spell of opera by immersing it in the sober factuality of concrete social conditions. The dogma of the identity of music and poetry inspired him with a fear of everything that resists such an identity, everything that can only be grasped as a shaped contrast to music. The alternation of music and text in *Fidelio* is far more political than the music dramas. And Wagner showed himself to be bourgeois through and through in his conviction that poetic depth is synonymous with the omission of historical specificity. His image of the universally human requires the dismantling of what he supposes to be relative and contingent in favour of the idea of an unvarying human nature. What is actually substantial appears to him as a residue. He therefore finds himself reduced to a stratum of subject-matter that acknowledges neither history nor the supernatural nor even the natural, but which lies beyond all such categories. Essence is drawn into an omnisignificant immanence; the immanent is held in thrall by symbol. This stratum, where all is undifferentiated, is that of myth. Its sign is ambiguity; its twilight is a standing invitation to merge irreconcilables—the positivistic with the metaphysical—because it firmly rejects both the transcendental and the factual. Gods and men perform on the same stage. After *Lohengrin*, Wagner actually banned authentic historical conflicts from his work. The world of chivalry in *Tristan* and *Parsifal* provides only the emotional colouring of a reality that has receded into the mists of time, and the exception of *The Mastersingers* really does just prove the rule. The mythical music drama is secular and magical at one and the same time. This is how it solves the riddle of the phantasmagoria.

However, the attempt to legitimate this hybrid form by appealing to the multiple meanings inherent in the myths has its

---

[2] The movement of liberal, radical writers associated with Heine—Gutzkow, Wienbarg, Laube and Mundt. Their writings were banned by edict in 1835. *Translator's note.*

limits. If Wagner's idea of an unvarying human nature turns out to be an ideological delusion then that delusion will be destroyed by the power of the myths as these assert themselves in his works against his will. The elective affinity that impels him towards the myths undermines the humanity in which he still believes: staunch bourgeois as he is, his conception of himself crumbles before his very eyes. No doubt his impotence benefits to a certain extent from the negative truth, from a dawning awareness of the chaos underlying the bourgeois order—but it is to this chaos that he is inexorably drawn back. This is the objective reason for Wagner's regression. The pure human being turns out to be an ideal projection of the savage who finally emerges from the bourgeois, and he celebrates him as if, metaphysically, he really were the pure human being. With whatever justice Wagner's music may be called psychological, the same claim can scarcely be made for his texts, which merely re-enact at a primitive, literal level those vestiges of the imagination that live on in the psychological subject. The dramatist of the *Ring*, and in effect all the mature works, scorns to 'develop' his characters. The Wagnerian tendency towards exteriorization, which always subordinates subjective animation to the tangible gesture and the outward effect, thereby manages to expose something of the ephemeral nature of subject-ivity itself. The motives of the characters are presented with almost exaggerated bluntness. Their behaviour changes with lightning rapidity. They barely retain their identity, and Siegfried is not even fully aware of his identity, as we can see from his frequent use of the impersonal instead of the personal pronoun— 'someone spoke'. Love is something that occurs only at first sight and never as inward stillness; this was the case as early as the *Dutchman*, and it applies with equal truth to Siegmund and Sieglinde and to Walther and Eva. The fact that, for all his German nationalist ideals, Wagner always remains free from a stuffy philistinism is something he owes to an unspoilt view of sex. This alone allows him to create the moving scene in which Brünnhilde wishes to preserve her maidenhood for the sake of her beloved, but where she yet gives herself without restraint.[3] Of course, her love

[3] *Siegfried*, Act III, sc. 3.

later changes to hate with equal rapidity. No reflection leads her to see through the mechanics of the intrigue; and later still, after Siegfried's death, her hate is as abruptly transformed back into love—here, too, without any attempt to resolve the logic of the plot. Once Gutrune has told her about the potion that made Siegfried forget her, she wastes no further time on it. It is as if Wagner had anticipated Freud's discovery that what archaic man expresses in terms of violent action has not survived in civilized man, except in attenuated form, as an internal impulse that comes to the surface with the old explicitness only in dreams and madness.

At the same time, however, Wagner's indifference towards the inner life of the individual reveals traces of a political awareness of the way the individual is determined by material reality. Like the great philosophers he mistrusts the private. His preoccupation with totality is not just totalitarian and administrative; it points also to the fact that the universe is an interlocking system in which the more ruthlessly the individual tries to prevail, the less he succeeds. The attempt to change the world comes to nought, but changing the world is what is at issue. Siegfried does not suffer from the Oedipus complex; instead he smashes Wotan's spear. If in the historical world the primordial conflict is sublimated into dream, in the Alberich-Hagen scene in *The Twilight of the Gods*, the transition takes place visibly on the stage. This concrete sensuousness, and its implied contrast with inwardness, stamps the mythological subject-matter with the mark of history to a much greater degree than Wagner's aesthetics would have us believe. Myth and culture succeed each other in phases, and in this way the mythic origins of culture come into view. As a dramatist Wagner can see how myth and law interlock. The 'contrasts' to which the *Ring*, following Schopenhauer, attaches such importance are predicated on anarchy. The war of all against all is resolved only with difficulty by the legal order emerging from it. It constantly breaks out anew wherever no explicit system of contracts exists to prevent it. Wotan is ready for any act of violence as long as he is not bound by codified agreements. Moreover, these very agreements, which impose restrictions on an unenlightened state of nature, turn out to be fetters that deprive him of the freedom of movement and hence help to re-establish chaos. In Wagner, law is unmasked as the equivalent of lawlessness. The *Ring* could have as its motto the statement by Anaximander recently analysed by Heidegger, who as a mythologist of language is not unlike Wagner: 'Wherever existing things have their origin, there too they must of necessity perish, for they must pay the penalty and be condemned for their iniquity, in accordance with the order of time.'[4] The law that defined itself as punishment for lawlessness comes to resemble it and itself becomes lawlessness, an order for destruction: that, however, is the nature of myth as it is echoed in pre-Socratic thought, and Wagner adopts it not just as subject-matter, but in its innermost aesthetic consequences. The archaic idea of Fate presides over the seamless web of universal immanence in the *Gesamtkunstwerk*, and in all likelihood it also provides the foundation for the musical principle enshrined in the notion of 'the art of transition', of universal mediation. Wagner's music conforms to the law that tension and resolution should, in the main, correspond to one another, that nothing should be left unbalanced or allowed to stand out aloof and isolated: in his eyes all musical being is Being-for-another, it is 'socialized' in the process of composition itself. No doubt all bourgeois musical treatment of consonance and dissonance aimed at something of the sort, but in Wagner the law of the symmetry of tension and resolution becomes a specific part of his technical canon. Schoenberg, who was the first composer to question this principle, was nevertheless able as a theoretician to discover the authentic formula for it, in a strictly Wagnerian spirit: 'Every tone which is added to a beginning tone makes the meaning of that tone doubtful. If, for instance, G follows after C, the ear may not be sure whether this expresses C major or G major, or even F major or E minor; and the addition of other tones may or may not clarify this problem. In this manner there is produced a state of unrest, of imbalance which grows throughout most of the piece, and is enforced further by similar functions of the rhythm. The method by which balance is restored seems to me the real idea of the composition.'[5]

In creating that 'balance' the balance of Fate is also struck; all that

---

[4] Adorno quoted Anaximander in Nietzsche's translation. *Translator's note.*
[5] Arnold Schoenberg, *Style and Idea*, New York 1950, p. 49.

has happened is retracted, and the legal order established in art becomes the restitution of the primal condition. With complete consistency and, incidentally, with superlative insight into the logic of the process of composition, Schoenberg speaks in a different passage of the motival and harmonic obligations that the finished composition has to satisfy.[6] This establishes the primacy of exchange over the organization and internal progression of the work of art: it becomes the incarnation of the processes of exchange in society as a whole. With this regression to myth, bourgeois society salutes itself by name in Wagner: all novel events in music measure themselves against their predecessors and by cancelling them out the new is itself constantly cancelled out. The origin is reached with the liquidation of the whole. The realization that late bourgeois society possesses these anarchist features decodes the totality as a prehistoric anarchy. This anarchy is still repudiated by Wagner the bourgeois, but it is already desired by Wagner the musician. If in the *Ring* mythic violence and legal contract are confounded, this not only confirms an intuition about the origins of legality, it also articulates the experience of the lawlessness of a society dominated in the name of law by contract and property. The aesthetic criticism of Wagner, that as a modern he had violated the ancient and, as a profane person, offended against myth, may well be justified. But, equally, it must be pointed out that a regressive aesthetic practice is not a matter of individual choice or psychological accident. He belongs to the first generation to realize that in a world that has been socialized through and through it is not possible for an individual to alter something that is determined over the heads of men. Nevertheless, it was not given to him to call the overarching totality by its real name. In consequence it is transformed for him into myth. The opacity and omnipotence of the social process is then celebrated as a metaphysical mystery by the individual who becomes conscious of it and yet ranges himself on the side of its dominant forces. Wagner has devised the ritual of permanent catastrophe. His unbridled individualism utters the death sentence on the individual and its order.

As he searches for the cause of his own entanglement in the

[6] Cf. ibid., p. 67.

ground of the world, an understanding is reached between the present and the mythical. Wagner has not conjured up the myths simply as metaphors: beneath his gaze everything becomes mythological, and this applies with particular force to the only modern subject he ever treated. *The Mastersingers* flirts with that convention that used to operate in painting, according to which pictures of events remote in time and space could be peopled with the inhabitants of the modern world. The woman from Nuremberg is dispatched to John the Baptist on the Jordan.[7] An endless tradition of *Kitsch* has attached itself at second hand to such Wagnerian allegorizing. But the anachronism is more than a pretended naivety and a pleasure in archaizing pastiche. In that light-hearted opera every element of the present sounds as if it were a reminiscence. The expression of sweet nostalgia merges with the allure of the familiar, the promise of security at home, together with the feeling, 'When was I here before?', and the archetypes of the bourgeois find themselves invested with the nimbus of what is long since past. Ultimately, the work captivates its audience much more because of this than because of its nationalist self-idolization and its bestial sense of humour. Each listener has the feeling that it belongs to him alone, that it is a communication from his long-forgotten childhood, and from this shared *déjà vu* the phantasmagoria of the collective is constructed. The atmosphere distilled in this witches' kitchen is irresistible because it stirs up, gratifies and even legitimates ideologically an impulse that adult life has only laboriously and not wholly successfully managed to master. It relaxes everyone's limbs, not just Sachs's, and, as the demagogue of the feelings, the composer demonstrates the right reactions in which everyone then joins. Nowhere is Wagner more mythological than in the modernity of such pleasures. He can adapt to the most subtle nuances of individuality, but he does so in order to prepare the listener for the amorphous bliss of a pre-individual condition. The promise of happiness that gingerbread holds out to the Nuremberger is shown to be a divine realm of ideas. Whatever truth this contains, however, is subordinated to a lie. Wagner fraudulently presents

[7] See *The Mastersingers*, Act III, sc. I.

the historical German past as its essence. In this way he has invested concepts such as 'ancestors' and 'the people' with that absoluteness which was subsequently unleashed in an outburst of absolute horror. This manipulated awakening of memory is the exact opposite of enlightenment. Spitzweg's poetry of the cultural landscape[8] cannot help mocking its eccentrics and deviants, and in the same way we find in Wagner a strange confusion of the moonlit night and the smell of lilac (whose romantic charm was unknown in the sixteenth century) with sadistic brutality. The lambent quality of the music, the tone of the *Venusberg*, encourages its hearers to cast off not just their mundane reality, but also their humanity, and to give free rein to their destructive impulses. With the diabolical relish that is inseparable from the simple good humour it claims to be, the theatre-goer who takes pleasure in the brawl at the end of Act II is really gloating at a miniature foretaste of the violence to come.

All Wagnerian ambiguity stems from his relationship to archaic images. His talent for calling up the past pursues the inflections of the soul down to their real models and so illuminates their regressive element; at the same time, however, he entrusts himself to this element as if it were primordial truth and so he regresses too. Aesthetically he anticipates tensions that became explicit only with the disagreements between Freud and Jung. His 'psychoanalytic' motifs—incest, hatred of the father, castration—have been pointed out often enough; and Sachs's apothegm about 'true dream interpretation'[9] seems to bring the work of art close to the analytic ideal of making the unconscious conscious. At moments of the process of becoming conscious, Wagner's language anticipates that of Nietzsche thirty years before *Zarathustra*:

> Descend then, Erda, Great Mother of fear,
> Great Mother of sorrow!
> Away, away to eternal sleep![10]

[8] Carl Spitzweg (1806–1885) specialized in paintings of eccentric characters like the bookworm or the poet in the attic. *Translator's note.*

[9] 'All poetry and the art of verse / Is nothing but true dream interpretation.' *The Mastersingers*, Act III, sc. 2. *Translator's note.*

[10] *Siegfried*, Act III, sc. 1.

And from the same perspective Siegfried replies:

> Bravery or bravado—how do I know![11]

However, the formula is itself mythical. The gesture of challenge contained in that 'bravery and bravado' comes to resemble the archaic powers, and the 'how do I know?', with its persistent blankness, easily succumbs to them once again. Siegfried is not just the individual laboriously freeing himself from an unconscious state of nature. He is already the fool who will be celebrated in *Parsifal*, the 'childish hero' the 'idiot', who does not overcome fear by achieving a knowledge of self, but who merely does 'not know' what fear is, and when he finds out, from his experience of sex, forgets it again. When Wotan dismisses Erda, the Great Mother of fear, she does not lose her power and neither does he gain his liberty. On the contrary, in the Norn scene[12] he succumbs to their sentence against his will and the Norns descend to the Great Mother when the rope snaps. The only function of consciousness is to complete the circle of unconsciousness. The cosmogonist Klages rejects Wagner; but there is more of his philosophy in the Erda passages than there is of psychoanalysis. Even his theory of knowledge, the notion of drifting organic images as opposed to conscious thought, is to be found in rudimentary form in *Siegfried*. Erda's sleep is said to be 'brooding' and she says of herself:

> My sleep is dreaming,
> My dreaming meditation,
> My meditation mastery of wisdom.[13]

As in Klages, the disenfranchisement of the earth signifies metaphysical calamity:

> I am confused since I awoke:
> Wildly and awry the world revolves![14]

[11] Ibid., Act II, sc. 2.
[12] *The Twilight of the Gods*, Prelude.
[13] *Siegfried*, Act III, sc. 1.
[14] Ibid.

Whoever takes action against blind fate stands condemned as the demonic antagonist of the soul: the world ash-tree is mortally wounded by the God who cut his spear from it. It is Wagner who starts the process of transforming Schopenhauer's metaphysical concept of the Will into the more manageable theory of the collective unconscious. Ultimately this turns into the 'soul of the people', in which a brutality borrowed from the overbearing individual combines in an explosive mixture with the amorphous masses who have been solicitously protected from any thoughts of an antagonistic society. It is only logical for the Wagnerian mythology to pass into the iconography of the Wilhelmine world: the signal sounded by the Emperor's horn was a simplified version of Donner's motiv in the *Ring*.

It is impossible to overlook the relationship between Wagnerian mythology and the iconic world of the Empire, with its eclectic architecture, fake Gothic castles, and the aggressive dream symbols of the Neo-German boom, ranging from the Bavarian castles of Ludwig to the Berlin restaurant that called itself 'Rheingold'. But the question of authenticity is as fruitless here as elsewhere. Just as the overwhelming power of high capitalism forms myths that tower above the collective conscious, in the same way the mythic region in which the modern consciousness seeks refuge bears the marks of that capitalism: what subjectively was the dream of dreams is objectively a nightmare. To that extent it can be asserted that the inauthentic aspect of that iconic world, namely the distortion of the myths at the hands of later generations who discover themselves and mirror themselves in them, is also its truth. Confronted with an exorbitant unapproachable world of things that casts its alien shadow over him, the individual feels an affinity with the world of myth. What he shares with it is the gesture of falling silent. For all his rhetoric and perhaps even for its sake, this gesture is in fact of crucial importance for Wagner. Newman has pointed out the similarity between the poem of the *Ring* and Vischer's *Vorschlag zu einer Oper* (Suggestion for an Opera). [15] The philosopher of aesthetics postulates a Nibelung opera, arguing that the myth of the Nibelungs, to which in the

[15] Cf. Newman, Vol. 2, pp. 158, 170, 231 et passim.

Romantic manner he attributes all the substantial qualities of the German character, resists the spoken drama because of the taciturnity of its characters. This taciturnity can be both retained and overcome by means of music. If we think of the *Ring* as the implementation of Vischer's suggestion—according to Newman it is certain that Wagner was acquainted with it—what he has done is not to break down the silence of myth, but to introduce music into it. The function of music as 'accompaniment' in the tetralogy is not just a stylistic principle; it is essential for the dramatic characters. As representatives of ideas they are actually too empty to have anything to 'express', so it is not for nothing that Wagner's expressiveness operates sparingly with a reservoir of typical characters from stock. The composer as it were absolves his characters from the necessity of being individuals, of having their own souls: they do not sing, they just recite their roles. As puppets wriggling in the hands of the World Spirit who manipulates them in the spirit of technical rationality, they come close in spirit to the object-oriented, subjectively impoverished characters of the original *Lay of the Nibelungs*, where the narrator's presence remains in the foreground and the characters are consigned to a secondary role. Expression and an inner life are in general not birds of a feather and it sometimes seems as though the self-postulating, self-reflecting expression were attempting to recover through imitation something already lost. The Wagnerian *espressivo* removes from his characters something that in any case they possessed as little as figures on a film screen; 'the poet speaks' because Fate strikes them dumb. And by taking sides with a Fate suspended over the powerless, music renounces its profoundest critique, its critique of myth, something that had been implicit in music throughout the entire period of bourgeois ascendancy, ever since the invention of the opera as a form. By identifying with myth, it identifies ultimately with its falseness. In Wagner's musical theatre the figure of Orpheus is unimaginable, just as in his version of the Nibelung story there is no room for Volker, although the scene where the minstrel plays his violin to serenade the Burgundians to sleep on their last night was better suited than any other to give birth to music. The true idea of opera, that of a solace that forces open the gates of the underworld, has been lost. Such solace would entail a caesura in the musical flow, but wherever Wagner's sense of form leads him to write in that vein, as in the quintet of Act III of *The Mastersingers*, which begins with a new theme, his creativity mysteriously dries up. After a few bars of a tender, luminous beauty the passage falls back on the stock of motivs of the Prize Song. It fails to develop from the new idea and is rounded off only formally: an impotent gesture, though, admittedly, all the more moving for that fact. Otherwise the music simply follows the action without ever transcending it. The music dramas are in reality not operas at all; all that survives of the opera proper is the hieratic element that had always belonged to it and which reaches a climax in *Fidelio* as the ritual of bourgeois liberty. That Wagner knew this to be the case is borne out by descriptions like *Bühnenfestspiel* (stage festival) and *Bühnenweihfestspiel* (festival performance for the consecration of the stage). All tension is removed from the operas by the element of 'consecration'. It is as if they were repeatable acts of worship. They abandon themselves to the pure immanent flow of the action, weeding out otherness in any form, in short, eliminating freedom. Nowhere is Wagner more mythical and heathen than in this very consecration, a vain attempt to recapture the essence of the mystery play. It follows from this that words and music have the same meaning for Wagner. In an astounding insight, Vischer excluded Beethoven from his programme for a mythic opera, because he was 'too symphonic'. All myth is annihilated by the character of 'Oh Hope, let not thy last faint star',[16] and in fact every bar in Beethoven transcends the natural order from which it arises and with which it becomes reconciled. In the same way, the symphonic form, what Schoenberg called 'developing variation', is the anti-mythological principle par excellence. In Wagner, however, nature is not conciliated but mastered, and this is why its verdict has the final word. For all the protestations in his theoretical writings, the innermost heart of his work is as unsymphonic as his use of motivs: the key to any artistic content lies in its technique.

---

[16] 'Oh Hope, let not thy last faint star in dark despair be blinded.' This comes in Leonore's aria 'Abscheulicher, wo weilst du hin' in Act I of *Fidelio*. *Translator's note.*

The changed relationship of music to its content is reflected with particular sharpness in the case of Wagner's poetry, in its relation to the fairy-tale. This lapses into myth. The texts are full of fairy-tale motifs, such as the reality that steps out of a picture—the *Dutchman*—or out of a story—*Lohengrin* and the Siegfried of Act I of *The Twilight of the Gods*. Such things are found in Grimm, for example in the *Robber Bridegroom*. This rupturing of the logic of the image entails nothing less than the suspension of the myth. So powerful are such impulses in *Lohengrin* that they frustrate the overall scheme of the play: the work is 'complete' at the end of Act I, just as the *Dutchman* is essentially complete at the moment of the hero's meeting with Senta. Act II is not the logical sequel to the phantasmagoria of Act I, but just an epic continuation. The mature Wagner operates generally with a kind of 'epic theatre'. The abandonment of any tension between music and myth means that tragedy is sacrificed from the outset. The determinism of form and action knows of conflict only as an illusion, as the self-deception of characters labouring under a misapprehension. This is why the musical flow is able simply to absorb everything that takes place. The texts particularly and the musical organization are of one mind in this respect. And the goal they strive for is the triumph of myth over fairy-tale. This is perfectly obvious from the history of the motif of the man who knew no fear. Newman reports[17] that in his revolutionary days in Dresden Wagner had wanted to compose an opera based entirely on the Grimm fairy-tale. Then he suddenly identified the hero of the tale with the mythical Siegfried.[18] The fairy-tale element posed the greatest difficulties for Wagner, above all in the construction of the *Ring*. They could not be overcome in the three versions of *Siegfried* Act I and their repercussions may still be seen in certain inconsistencies in the final version.[19] In terms of the drama, these focus upon Siegfried's fearless spontaneity—the man without fear is he over whom neither the father's spell nor the natural order of the generations has any power. The problem is that this fearlessness cannot be made to harmonize with Mime's plans and calculations. The plot cannot make up its mind whether

[17] Newman, Vol. 2, p. 337n.
[18] Ibid.
[19] Ibid., pp. 35–6.

it is Siegfried's fear or his fearlessness that Mime, the foolishly cunning instrument of fate, should try to exploit. The transcendental implications of the fairy-tale world, that which in Wotan's word 'is different' and not eternal sameness, refuse to be integrated into the natural and social order. They can only be smuggled in at some blind spot. An instance is Act I of *Siegfried*, in Mime's poorly motivated and unconvincing vision of terror. The regression of fairy-tale into myths leaves behind it scars that bear witness to Wagner's frustrated attempt to break out.

In sacrificing the fairy-tale to what has existed from time immemorial, Wagner's work allows itself to be appropriated by bourgeois ideology. Myth becomes mythologizing; the power of what simply exists becomes its own legitimation. The links connecting bourgeois ideology to myth can be seen at their clearest in *Lohengrin* where the establishment of a sacrosanct sphere inviolable by any profane tampering coincides directly with the transfiguration of bourgeois arrangements. In line with the authentic spirit of ideology, the subjugation of women in marriage is dressed up as humility, as the achievement of a pure love. Male professional life, which must of necessity be incomprehensible to women by virtue of their strict exclusion from it, appears as a sacred mystery. The Knight of the Swan bestows glory, where the husband merely disburses money; even earlier, the Dutchman had been a good match. Female masochism magically transforms the brutality of the husband's 'That concerns you not' into the fervent 'My lord, never shall this question come from me'.[20] The master's whims, his imperious commands, and above all the division of labour which Wagner overtly criticizes, are all unconsciously affirmed. The man who 'fights' for his means of existence out in the world becomes a hero, and after Wagner there were doubtless countless women who thought of their husbands as Lohengrins. In the course of the plot Elsa is forced to submit to such an idealization and nothing remains of her original vision. At first she rebels against the incomprehensible obligations of male professional life—a rebellion that echoes in the overtones of such stirring formulae as

[20] *Lohengrin*, Act I, sc. 2.

The Grail has sent for its loitering knight![21]

—and for which she is punished. Nor would she have it otherwise:

So that you may punish me, I lie here before you![22]

The vestiges of untamed feeling that proclaim themselves in this feminine protest are suppressed in the name of the miracles that kindle feminine admiration, and this fact unmasks the miracle as a lie. Hence Wagner's mythology ends in conformism. It is at this point that all defensive mockery of Wagner becomes justifiable. If the mythology strengthens bourgeois ideology, then the latter convicts the mythological ambitions of absurdity. In his condemnation of others, Wagner had invoked idiosyncratic responses to the elements of the trivial, the infantile or the merely individual in his own nature. The bridal chamber must be included in the list of intimate scenes that arouse disgust, if not mirth. Unabashed self-indulgence, the corollary of bourgeois self-discipline, results in the ludicrous nature-sounds of the Rhine Maidens and Valkyries, in Hans Sachs's 'Oho! Trallalei! O he', in such expressions of 'fervent' sexual passion as Brünnhilde's apostrophe of herself as 'wild passionate woman',[23] or in verses like

A delicious maw you display,
Teeth laughing in a dainty muzzle![24]

and last but not least, in Sachs's

Away to the meadow, put your best foot forward![25]

The inevitable response to such passages is embarrassment for the bourgeois who has ceased to be one. From here it is no great

[21] *Lohengrin*, Act III, sc. 3.
[22] Ibid.
[23] *Siegfried*, Act III, sc. 3.
[24] *Siegfried*, Act II, sc. 2.
[25] *The Mastersingers*, Act III, sc. 4.
[26] *The Valkyrie*, Act I, sc. 2 and sc. 3.

distance to the garrulousness and complacency that mar Wagner's work at every point. The demagogue talks his followers to death, and the unending melody follows suit. Such features merge with the over-familiarity; the behaviour of Wotan and even Gurnemanz is altogether too free and easy. Secrets that have long since become public are confided in gossipy detail; Sigmund declares with pathos that Volsa is his father even though he has previously addressed him as such.[26] Hunding instantly detects the resemblance between Sigmund and Sieglinde, yet the subsequent revelation that the two are brother and sister is supposed to shock. All this tries to justify itself by the argument that for primitive thought a fact is only a fact when it is given a name. In reality, however, all that is happening is that Wagner's own bonhomie is saluting itself, and its primal sounds are in Saxon dialect. The fact is that he is enjoying himself hugely. If the music drama lacks a redeeming word, this is made up for by the way in which the characters incessantly proclaim their redemption to each other. It is not only Elisabeth who desires to die 'pure and angelic', nor Eva who can thank Sachs with the words

> Only through you did I think
> Nobly, freely, boldly.[27]

It is not for nothing that the gestures of the most celebrated erotic artist of the bourgeois world should reflect back on themselves: they are narcissistic. In Wagner's invocation of mythology, the cult of the past and of the individual are inextricably intertwined. To this the *Ring of the Nibelungs* stands witness.

---

[27] *The Mastersingers*, Act III, sc. 4.

9

God and Beggar

In its form, the *Ring* is a metaphor of the totality of world history which perfects itself by achieving consciousness of what it had been in itself from time immemorial. If this reminds us as much of Hegel as of Schopenhauer, from whom Wagner borrowed the content of the allegory, then it remains true that beyond all this there is one particular aspect in which the *Ring* is in agreement with Hegel's philosophy of history. And this is the ruse of reason. Whatever opposition there is to the totality, to Wotan's universal will, is also in accord with it, because Wotan's absolute spirit has nothing in mind but its own annihilation. Thus as early as Siegmund we find these verses:

> The crisis calls for a hero
> who, free from divine protection,
> will be released from divine law.
> So he alone will be fit to do the deed
> which, much as the gods need it,
> a god is nevertheless prevented from doing.[1]

This is repeated in the case of Siegfried: the final judgment on world history, which Siegfried is preparing to implement, can only be carried out by those who, like him, are ignorant and are exempt from the mythic yoke of contract and property.

> I can offer neither land nor people,
> nor father's house and palace:

[1] *The Valkyrie*, Act II, sc. 1.

> I inherited only my own body,
> and that I consume as I live.[2]

The Romanticized concept of the proletariat assigns the 'task of salvation' to the latter, because it is supposed to stand outside the nexus of social guilt, whilst suppressing the fact that it is dependent on the social mechanism. This Romantic concept is complemented here by the no less Romantic notion that society would be able to regenerate itself if only it could find its way back to its unsullied origins. Ultimately the regeneration theory emerges in *Parsifal* as a theory of a master caste. But even the anti-feudal *Ring*, in which it is tacitly implied, brings its dubious side to light. Because he is an unspoilt child of nature, Siegfried is able and willing to submit to a social demand that is negated and even concealed by his own asocial innocence: Wagner falsifies the condition of the disinherited by misrepresenting the oppressed man as the unmutilated one. By virtue of this misrepresentation, Siegfried becomes the servant of the cunning of actual existence and so ends up as the accomplice of the whole. As such, and as the embodiment, one could say, of a proletariat patterned on a woodcutter, he drives both himself and the whole to their ruin. Siegfried, once placed in this role, ceases to be the allegorical representative of a class; he is transformed into an 'individual', and hence into the chimera of the pure, unhistorical, immediate human being. The revolutionary turns into the rebel. All his opposition remains imprisoned within the system of bourgeois society because it does not evolve from actual social processes, but seems instead to come from outside, only to be sucked into the vortex.

The individualistic impulses that set out to oppose society are of the same dour type that determines the form of that society: in Hegel it is the 'passions', in Schopenhauer human 'needs', as the concrete shape of the Will in individuation. If the entire story of the *Ring* can be regarded as the history of Wotan's self-knowledge, which, having become conscious, withdraws from the world of action and negates itself, then any opposition to him must be as blind as the Will in itself and its blindness leads to death as certainly

---

[2] *The Twilight of the Gods*, Act I, sc. 2.

as knowledge does. The passion of the Volsungs pursues particular goals that are incompatible with the existing totality and which nevertheless hold out to that totality the only hope of success, the rule of Wotan. But because the Hegelian theory of the realization of reason in the world is missing, the structure of the *Ring* becomes as tangled as the threads held by the Norns. *The Twilight of the Gods* does not simply put Schopenhauer's metaphysical verdict into effect; it also signals Wagner's escape from a philosophy of history in which the antagonism between the universal and the particular constantly shimmers deceptively like a mirage. It is devoid of the dialectical articulation in which Hegel masters it, but it is no less devoid of any hope of an altered condition in which the recurrent antagonism might vanish. The fact that resistance is produced by the social totality has its corollary in the end, in the identification of resistance with domination: here is the outer limit of the power of the *Ring* to interpret history, and from there it seeps away into the void. The rebel of the particular becomes the executive organ of the totality; that is to say he destroys it without ever discovering a new, different totality. The totality itself, however, is the bad eternity of rebellion as anarchy and unrelenting self-destruction. There is in fact no real demarcation line separating Wotan, the father of the gods, and Siegfried, his lethal rescuer and the antagonist who succours him, and in their union the *Ring* celebrates the capitulation of the revolution that never was. With unsurpassed acuity, Semmig, Wagner's companion on his flight from Dresden in the moment when the revolution there had been defeated, observed this ambivalence directly: 'The paroxysm lasted perhaps more than half an hour; and so overwhelmed was I by the storm of words of this man sitting next to me—*shall I call him Wotan or Siegfried?*—that I could not address a single word to him.'[3] The embarrassment that Siegfried, the 'ruler of the world' should without demur become the servant of the Gibichungs, should lend himself to the Hagen intrigue and then submit to the fate that Wotan 'wills', at the same time that he is supposed to bend it according to *his* will, is painfully obvious, together with the ambiguity of the entire construction. This ambiguity is inscribed

[3] Quoted by Newman, Vol. 2, p. 95.

in the changing conceptions of the whole tetralogy. In the first version Siegfried perishes but manages to save Valhalla. In its final shape we are led to the despairing conclusion that in order to be something more than the victim and the servant of the existing order and yet unable to modify an existing reality from which he has sprung and to which he is recalled by Wagner's own spirit of resignation, Siegfried brings about not only his own destruction and that of individuation, but also the downfall of the whole.

This acquiescence on the part of the embodiment of unfettered power, the collapse of bourgeois revolution and the portrayal of the universal process as universal destruction—these motifs all come together in a murky witches' brew. Their interconnectedness, at least the relation between a failed insurrection and nihilistic metaphysics, has not, after Nietzsche, gone unnoticed. But at a much more profound level than that of the surface action, which could always appeal to its source, the mythical delusions of the Edda and the *Nibelungenlied*, we have to take note of the betrayal of the tetralogy's hero, Wotan. The image of Wotan is a puzzle made up of rebel and god, mythology and bourgeois society. Literally, in his image: that of the wanderer dressed in a long dark-blue cape, with a spear in his hand as a staff, and a round, broad hat with its rim turned down, who visits Mime, Alberich, Erda and Siegfried in turn. It is his figure of all in Wagner's work that descends to posterity as the bourgeois figure par excellence: the vigorous man, no longer young, with his slouch hat, his rain cloak—a havelock— full beard and spectacles reminding us that he only has one eye. In a satirical poem on the nationalistic petty bourgeois by Thoma, the editor of *Simplizissimus* who subsequently developed Pan-German views himself, we read:

> Hussa, Hoya, with giant stride
> I boldly from my office glide.

and later: 'The icy frost gives me no sores!' The cumulative force of such caricatures, however, is not connected with Wagner's bourgeois successors and followers, but derives from the bourgeois models that had originally come together to form the different 'roles' in the music dramas. Everything suggests that their characteristics are those of the fake German revolutionary of the type of *Turnvater* Jahn and the *Burschenschaften*, whom Marx had satirized.[4] The primitive Germans were once upon a time evoked as the patron saints of liberty, representing the healthy state of a lost paradise. Their ludicrous, half-paternal, half-authoritarian gestures were those of men who do not allow their actions to be prescribed by others. The nationalist beard expressed their rejection of courtly decorum, just as the slouch hat implied rejection of the top hat and the havelock pointed to their defiance of nature, something they could do with impunity because, as elemental beings, they were part of it. But if the 'German Socialists' were never socialists except in name, their allegorical transformation into the Wotan of the *Ring* signifies their reconciliation with the bourgeoisie: they have themselves become fathers, their anger rationalized as paternal punishment, just as their conciliatoriness is that of the father who wishes his oppressed child a good night and the world a good nothing. Their insurrection has vanished like a ghost, leaving nothing behind but its outward appearance. Wotan is the phantasmagoria of the buried revolution. He and his like roam around like spirits haunting the places where their deeds went awry, and their costume compulsively and guiltily reminds us of that missed opportunity of bourgeois society for whose benefit they, as the curse of an abortive future, re-enact the dim and distant past. The ghostly nature of Wotan is hinted at by Wagner, for the old god, shorn of his powers, can only 'walk abroad' like a spirit in the human world. He has lost his name and his home. Hence, like a ghost, he turns up unexpectedly, the spectral image of his own past omnipresence, with threatening mien and, having once appeared, 'approaches very slowly, a step at a time'. His unexpected appearance terrifies Mime, and later on makes Siegfried laugh as at a strange relic. His leitmotiv is reminiscent of lullabies, as if his archaic physical self had been reduced to a shadow and relegated to the realm of dream, a fate which also befalls Alberich. His enharmonic chords serve as a metaphor for the paradox that the

---

[4] The *Burschenschaften* were the student societies that sprang up at the end of the Napoleonic Wars strongly influenced by the radical nationalism of Ludwig Jahn (1778–1852). His nickname *Turnvater* (gym-father) alludes to the important role he assigned to physical education as a means of invigorating the *Volk*.

immutable makes itself felt as shock. But there are many indications that, as the spirit of the ancient, now dispossessed god, the Wanderer is also the embodiment of the dispossessed but new revolution. Since the Wanderer only speaks, he necessarily drops out of the action; his aura arises from his position outside society. In this way he becomes the immediate prefiguration of the spectator of *The Twilight of the Gods* who has symbolically fallen silent. For this reason the indefatigable Mime, the representative of a reflectiveness that is practical, stupid and cunning all at once, judges his knowledge—'reason'—to be worthless:

> Many store up useless knowledge.[5]

The man who roams the world idly is the beggar.

> Many have greeted me with gifts,[6]

he says of himself, and the miserly Mime tries to chase him off with the words:

> I let loiterers go their way.[7]

He replies:

> No one nowadays can recognize God in the
> oft ragged beggar.

The threatening image of the beggar contains that of the rebel: by adopting the stance of the petitioner he has found himself a bourgeois home in Bohemian circles. The fact that this image colours that of the god means, in the first place, that the man who has been dispossessed and reduced to beggary is the man who had been a god—that he once had the opportunity to change the world and lost it. In the second place, it means that the rebel who appears as God thereby goes over to the side of authority and acts as the

---

[5] *Siegfried*, Act 1, sc. 2.
[6] Ibid.
[7] Ibid.

representative of the world that he ought to have changed. In this way Wotan becomes a sort of eery but amiable bogeyman, and the whole *Ring* may be described as an uninhibited lullaby for the bourgeoisie—with the refrain 'Rest, rest in peace O God'. In the scene with the Wanderer and Siegfried, Wagner enters the linguistic realm of children's verse. Siegfried interrogates the stranger as Red Ridinghood interrogates the wolf.

> But what do you look like?
> Why do you wear such a big hat?
> Why does it hang over your face like that?

And Wotan answers:

> That is the wanderer's way
> When he walks against the wind.[8]

The bonhomie of this reply, like that of all the Wanderer's utterances, has to be dissolved into its components. It ambiguously blends mundane bourgeois experience and mythical prehistory together: it is not for nothing that formally it smacks of the proverb—a trope that mediates between the oracle and healthy common sense. Mythical and doom-laden, Wotan's statement aims to conceal the truth about himself which is simultaneously revealed by the music in the Wanderer harmonies followed by the Valhalla motiv. At the same time the oracular revelation is true: it is the truth of the beggar to whose realm of experience it belongs. The 'that's the way it is' of proverbial speech is rooted in the pauper's acceptance of the world whose 'way' has always been thus, and the impotent man can only resign himself. But what has always been so finds a corresponding echo in the myth that clothes the god in immutable emblems. The wisdom of the experienced beggar dons the insignia of the primeval god. These, the 'practical' garments that protect the pauper from the natural forces to which society abandons him, are themselves age-old. And to cap it all, the bonhomie in which bourgeois and myth disguise each other has been, ever since Shakespeare's Iago, the true mark of the traitor. It

[8] *Siegfried*, Act III, sc. 2.

is reflected in the scene between the Wanderer and Siegfried. If we were to summarize the 'idea' of the *Ring* in simple words we would say that man emancipates himself from the blind identity with nature from which he springs; he then acquires power over nature only to succumb to her in the long run. The allegory of the *Ring* asserts that dominion over nature and subjugation by nature are one and the same. The division of the world into nature and individuation is parallel to the split between authority and rebels. In the scene with the Wanderer and Siegfried the profane substance of that metaphysical dualism becomes visible. Siegfried says:

> Old gossip do have done.

To which the Wanderer replies:

> Patience, my lad! If I seem old to you,
> Then you should show me some respect.

Siegfried:

> That's not bad!
> All my life an old man
> Has always stood in my way:
> Now I've swept him aside.[9]

To all appearances it is the disrespectful Siegfried who has come off best in this exchange. But to emerge the winner is also to succumb to the power of the Ring. The music leaves us in no doubt about this. Accompanying the Wanderer's last words, 'Forward then! I cannot stop you',[10] we hear the motiv of the twilight of the gods. The parable of the man who dominates nature only to relapse into a state of natural bondage gains an historical dimension in the action of the *Ring*: with the victory of the bourgeoisie, the idea that society is like a natural process, something 'fated', is reaffirmed, despite the conquest of particular aspects of nature. The catas-

[9] Ibid.
[10] Ibid.

trophe arises at the moment when this much-vaunted 'natural process' is revealed to be the mere product and stigma of an undirected social process and the lackey of an all-knowing authority. It is in this context that the musical gesture of retraction that lies at the heart of Wagner's music becomes fully comprehensible in social terms.

The betrayal is implicit in the rebellion. No late conversion to a conformist posture was required of the later Wagner; there was no need to repudiate his earlier insurrectionary values: his belief in the peasantry and in nothingness, in the void. We need only remind ourselves of the effect Bakunin had on him. In Newman's account Wagner describes Bakunin as follows: 'He cited . . . the delight, at once childlike and demoniac, of the Russian people in fire, on which Rostopchin had reckoned in his strategic burning of Moscow.' And Wagner's interpretation of anarchism is that all that is needed is 'to set in motion a world-wide movement to convince the Russian peasant—in whom the natural goodness of oppressed human nature had maintained itself in its most childlike form—that the burning of their lords' castles, with everything that was in and about them, was completely right in itself and pleasing in the sight of God; from this there must result the destruction of everything which, rightly considered, must appear even to the most philosophical thinkers of civilized Europe, the real source of all the misery of the modern world.'[11] Attachment to the soil and the magic of fire represent the most advanced beliefs of Wagner the politician. In the introduction to *Art and Revolution* he contrives with a certain amount of sophistry to distance himself from the concrete objectives of the insurrection in which he had taken part. 'But the greatest peril of all is that which the author would incur by his frequent use of the word "communism", should he venture into the Paris of today with these art-essays in his hand; for he openly proclaims his adherence to this severely scouted category, in contra-distinction to "egoism". I certainly believe that the friendly German reader, to whom the meaning of this antithesis will be obvious, will have no special trouble in overcoming the doubt as to whether he must rank me among the

[11] Newman, Vol. 2, p. 53.

partisans of the newest Parisian "*Commune*". Still, I cannot deny that I should not have embarked with the same energy upon the use of this word "communism" (employing it in a sense borrowed from the said writings of Feuerbach) as the opposite of egoism: had I not also seen in this idea a socio-political ideal which I conceived as embodied in a "*Volk*" [people] that should represent the incomparable productivity of antique brotherhood, while I look forward to the perfect evolution of this principle as the very essence of the associate manhood of the future.'[12] It is by no means the renegade we see at work here; instead the fine phrases of the renegade simply assert cynically what the rough voice of the bourgeois rebel had been at pains to conceal. Wagner's treachery is all of a piece with the bourgeois revolution itself. Paradoxically it is the pessimism of the *Ring* that contains an incipient criticism of that revolution in its implicit admission that the rebellion of Natural Man ends up in a reaffirmation of a social system that is seen as natural. And this insight is one that the ideological descendants of Wagner and his type of 'exaltation' would be reluctant to countenance, even if the swell of the orchestra in *The Twilight of the Gods* allowed them to perceive it. It is illuminating enough that Wagner reneged on his part in the revolution almost before the revolutionary events were at an end;[13] no less illuminating is the fact, demonstrated by Newman in detail, that official Wagner scholarship consciously and painstakingly falsified the account of his involvement.[14]

The conflict between rebellion and society is decided in advance in favour of society. In the *Ring*, the victory of society over the opposition and the recruitment of the latter for bourgeois purposes is idealized into a transcendental fate. Such an idealization alienates the allegory of world history from the actual historical process: 'What he had wanted to show was the inevitable decline of the world in its previous historical phase and to contrast this with Siegfried, the fearless, joyful man of the future. But as he came to carry out his plan, and indeed even in its initial conception, he was

[12] *Richard Wagner's Prose Works*, Vol. 1, pp. 27–8. By 'egoism' Wagner evidently means 'individualism'. *Translator's note.*
[13] Cf. Newman, Vol. 2, pp. 158, 170, 231 et passim.
[14] Cf. ibid., Vol. 2, pp. 9, 14, 18 et passim.

compelled to recognize that unconsciously he had been pursuing another and much deeper idea. What he had perceived in his poem, and what he has recognized in its essential senselessness, was not just a single phase of world history, but the nature of the world as such in all its conceivable phases.'[15] This is a textbook example of what Lukács once described as (trivialization through profundity:) by levelling down to the plane of the universally human and its 'senselessness', the true 'essence' of society—its actual historical laws of movement—is overlooked and the tragedy of a specific historical epoch is diluted into a universal principle. At the same time this tragedy is all too effective in the marks it leaves on the representatives of rebellion in the *Ring*. The opponents of order are isolated individuals wholly without true compassion, and devoid of any sense of solidarity. Siegfried, the man of the future, is a bully boy, incorrigible in his naivety, imperialistic in his bearing, equipped at best with the dubious merits of big-bourgeois self-confidence as contrasted with petty bourgeois pusillanimity. In Wagner there is hardly any humane collectivity, apart from the vague notion of the 'people'. The circle of singers in *Tannhäuser*, Hunding's clan, to a certain extent also the guilds in *The Mastersingers*—all are played down. In contrast to this, the glorified blood-brotherhood of *Parsifal* is the prototype of the sworn confraternities of the secret societies and *Führer*-orders of later years, which had so much in common with the Wahnfried circle—that clique held together by a sinister eroticism and its fear of the tyrant, with a hypersensitivity that bordered on terrorism towards everyone who did not belong. As its secret chief of police, Glasenapp in his great biography has drawn up formal lists of virtually every man and dog ever to come in contact with Wagner, and goes so far as to quibble because Nietzsche claimed Wagner as a friend of his merely because Wagner had called him *his* friend.[16] All relationships are distorted because they are integrated into a system of master and servant, a system disguised by concepts such as reverence and loyalty. Bayreuth even assumes some of the features of a rival government, which calls to mind the later

[15] Glasenapp, Vol. 3, Leipzig 1905, p. 50.
[16] Cf. Glasenapp, Vol. 5, Leipzig 1907, p. 388.

principle that the State must be subject to the Party. Such features may explain both Wagner's hostility towards Bismarck and the private claim to exclusivity, as well as the branding of deviant opinion as disloyalty. In the midst of liberal culture the aim was to set up a cultural monopoly; the taint of this sullies the purity of Wagner's criticism of the commercialization of the arts. According to Newman's evidence, the whole conception of Bayreuth is inseparable from the wire-pullings designed to eliminate the competition from the repertory theatre. The posthumous proposal for a Lex Parsifal reveals the truth about something implicit from the outset in the Wagnerian desire to renew the theatre. [17] The need to stifle any awareness of the element of usurpation and parasitism in his own clique meant that the sublime was all the more merciless in its judgments on the vulgar.

Nevertheless, in the midst of this distorted view of community, we gain a glimpse of the critical perspective from which the authentic face of society is ruthlessly exposed. Even the entanglement of world history in myth in the *Ring* is something more than the expression of a determinist metaphysics; it also makes possible a critique of a badly determined world. The Wagnerian resolution of all conflicts in advance is a measure of the web of illusions in bourgeois society, whose power is at its greatest at the moments when bourgeois ideology imagines it has achieved some consciousness of itself. Siegfried's love for Brünnhilde fades away on two separate occasions at the very moment when he utters her name. Brünnhilde, despite her knowledge, ignores Waltraut's warnings as does Siegfried those of the Rhine Maidens: it appears almost as though the most powerful impulse in the rebellious couple is that of self-immolation, the same urge which like a magnet draws Tristan and Isolde out of the daytime world that Siegfried and Brünnhilde set out to overcome. It is at this very point that Wagner's criticism of the bourgeois revolution breaks the surface. In his view there is no escape from the delusions of bourgeois

[17] The idea of Lex Parsifal was to restrict the performance of the opera to Bayreuth on the grounds that its 'earning power' would be greatly reduced if other theatres were allowed to produce it. A staging of *Parsifal* at the Metropolitan Opera House in New York in 1903 provoked an outcry among Wagnerians. *Translator's note.*

142

society as long as private property is retained. Within the system dominated by private property there can be no reconciliation between subjective pleasure—love [*Minne*]—and the objective, organized reproduction of life in society. In *Rhinegold*, the meaning of 'power', the Wagnerian antithesis of love, is simply the ability to dispose of the labour of others, admittedly with the implied condemnation of a 'grasping' capitalism. When the Rhine Maidens offer Siegfried his last chance, he rejects it with an appeal to the ultimate shibboleth, the formula of private property. When they call on him to give them the ring, the surrender of which would save both him and the world, he replies:

> If I were to waste what I have on you
> My wife would certainly scold me.[18]

When they laugh at him for his bourgeois attitude and threaten him, the ideological delusion is re-established in the mind of the man who has not learnt fear in a world where there is cause to fear everything. In Wagner, the bourgeoisie dreams of its own destruction, conceiving it as its only road to salvation even though all it ever sees of the salvation is the destruction. To the reified bourgeois world and to Fricka, the exponent of its morality, the revolution is described by Wotan as 'what spontaneously occurs'.[19] Organic life, however, which is thereby invoked as a corrective, remains blindly and aimlessly entangled in itself. Only Fate occurs spontaneously. In the *Ring* it is for the sake of Fate that mankind abandons all hope.

---

[18] *The Twilight of the Gods*, Act III, sc. 1.

[19] Cf. *The Valkyrie*, Act II, sc. 1. The spontaneous occurrence is the incestuous love of Siegmund and Sieglinde, which Wotan urges Fricka to accept. *Translator's note.*

10

Chimera

Wagner's pessimism is the philosophy of the apostate rebel. What he retains from his rebellion is his insight into the evil nature of the world 'as such', as an extrapolation from an evil present, as well as the further insight into the inexorable reproduction of that evil. He defects from rebellion simply by elevating this process to the status of an all-embracing metaphysical principle. As something immutable to all eternity, it derides all efforts to alter it and acquires the reflected glory of a dignity which it witholds from man. The metaphysical principle of meaninglessness is hypostatized into the meaning of empirical existence in exactly the same way as, later on, in German Existentialist philosophy. Faced with the conflict between individual interest and the total life process, he can only capitulate, and this surrender is celebrated as an act of state. It is doubtless a fact that, in the age of imperialism, 'idealism' renounced the power needed to bring about a 'reconciliation' between the irreducible antagonisms in bourgeois society, and criticism renders these starkly apparent. But Wagner renounces not only the illusory reconciliation, but also the attempt to overcome the contradiction, and, by sleight of hand, this abdication is transformed into the ground of the world. The notion of 'eternal justice' had been dubious enough in Schopenhauer, since its right to exist in the realm of the 'Idea', in the actual world, was disputed, while it was retained in the realm of the 'Will', where the only measuring-rod was the constancy of suffering and the diabolical belief that everything that exists is evil enough to deserve whatever fate befalls it.[1] In Wagner, however, this eternal

[1] Cf. Schopenhauer, *Sämtliche Werke* (Grossherzog Wilhelm Ernst Ausgabe), Leipzig n.d., Vol. 1, *Die Welt als Wille und Vorstellung* I, p. 464.

justice is twisted out of all recognition into reverence towards a
destiny that no longer even allows freedom a corrective role
within the realm of the Thing-in-itself, but instead consigns it
unceremoniously to the plane of farce. When Wotan denies
himself the will to live—

> I give up my work. Only one thing I want now:
> The end, the end!'[2]

—then, in strict contrast to Schopenhauer, even the self-denial of
the will has ceased to be an act of freedom. Freedom, even if only in
Schopenhauer's limited sense of a 'negative determinant', has no
place in Wagner. Wotan's denial of the will invokes a deterministic
universe that is illustrated metaphysically by Erda and the Norns,
and empirically by social contracts:

> I became ruler through treaties;
> By my treaties I am now enslaved.[3]

His renunciation not only enables him to escape from the trammels
of the world, but also, with Siegfried's death, leads him back into an
even deeper complicity with it. Where Schopenhauer pronounces
judgment on life as the blind game of the Will, Wagner obediently
submits to it, worshipping it as the sublime order of nature beyond
mortal comprehension. This makes possible his much-acclaimed
'positive' modification of Schopenhauer's philosophy by grafting
onto it the theory of regeneration with its racist overtones, a
development which, incidentally, played a part in estranging
Nietzsche from Schopenhauer.[4]

Mere impulse is transformed into the mysterious precept of a
now sanctified Mother Earth. Anything running counter to this in
the *Ring* is itself chthonic and impotent. The archaizing nature-
sounds associated with Erda and the Twilight of the Gods have an
affirmative function, which takes the place of that 'turning around'

[2] *The Valkyrie*, Act II, sc. 1.
[3] Ibid.
[4] Cf. Heinrich Rickert, *Philosophie des Lebens*, Tübingen 1922, p. 19.

or denial of the Will; they have a tranquillizing effect very different from that in Schopenhauer. For in fact it is not the Will that is negated in Wagner, but only the objectification of the Will in the Idea, in the phenomenal world. The Will itself, in other words the essence of the undirected social process, continues to be accepted in a spirit of compliant admiration. The individual then acquiesces without demur in his own annihilation, deeming it the work of that Will which has ceased to oppose itself to itself as Nature, but simply remains suspended unarticulated in a vacuum: every concrete yardstick by which to judge existing reality vanishes. But this is only possible because the negation of the Will has been wholly distorted. In Wagner the law of nature is no longer 'turned around' in the individual; on the contrary, the individual simply implements it. Logically this must bring Wagner into express contradiction to Schopenhauer. For the latter the 'turning around' of the Will-to-Life is synonymous with the process by which the Idea becomes conscious of itself. The Idea renounces its own Will-to-Life as a consequence of its recognition of the injustice which is the inevitable concomitant of the Will. It thereby breaks the vicious circle of a blind fate—Schopenhauer speaks of a circular track of red-hot coals from which it is essential to escape—in the hope that as a consequence of such behaviour the world with its burden of original sin will at last find peace. The first requirement of such renunciation is sexual asceticism. Now, Wagner does indeed accept this condition in *Parsifal*, but only to replace it with the worldly glory of the Grail community and chivalry, a price which in terms of Schopenhauer's philosophy could only be profoundly compromising. In the *Ring*, however, and in *Tristan*, the ascetic ideal is itself confused with sexual desire. The gratification of instinct and the negation of the Will-to-Life are jumbled together in a moment of rapture, in that 'laughing death' of Siegfried and Brünnhilde, in the night of love that should bring obliviousness of life:

> Take me up into thy arms
> Cut me from this hated world![5]

[5] *Tristan*, Act II, sc. 2.

When, finally, Tristan curses love, the object of the curse is the unquenchable longing for individuation, something that can be 'appeased' in the peace of death and in pleasure. While for Wagner pleasure assumes the features of death and destruction, in return death is celebrated in the mirror of the work as 'soaring joy' and greatest good. Its very lustre serves as an advertisement for death. In Schopenhauer, suffering appears as a 'mere phenomenon', its very shabbiness and meanness make its seriousness evident. In Wagner it is trivialized by the accoutrements of grandeur. It comes across as a material reality only when it afflicts dumb creatures, such as the swan in *Parsifal*. The prevention of cruelty to animals becomes sentimental as soon as compassion turns its back on mankind. Elsewhere, whenever it is allowed at all, suffering is diluted and reduced to the symbol of the unquenchable longing of the Will itself. Those wan, sickly heroes of Wagner—Tannhäuser, the Tristan of Act III, Amfortas—are all such symbols and their pallor is more like the protective colouring of an infinite all-consuming passion than the mark of the finite torment of human misery. Nothing remains of the reality of the 'Hell' which is how Schopenhauer conceived of the World as Idea.[6]

Many of Wagner's heroes perish without physical pain, and indeed without any explanation other than that of the exigencies of the plot. Tannhäuser, Elsa, Isolde and Kundry spring to mind. The defining feature of Siegfried's death is that he 'opens his eyes, radiantly', and as he dies he awakens to an awareness of Brünnhilde. Brünnhilde's death on a funeral pyre is nothing but a piece of Indian ostentation. In the teeth of the cult of the prevention of cruelty to animals, she even insists that her horse should neigh with joy as it leaps into the flames. Fear is repressed and becomes farce; only the sub-human Mime can scream 'ouch!' when he is beaten. In the spotlight of speculative death compassion can find no hiding-place, and it is steadfastly denied to all those who lay claim to it. In its place we find a total determinism that is used to engineer the exoneration of the main characters. Thanks to the potions of love and forgetfulness, Tristan and Siegfried are, as it were, relieved of those civic responsibilities from which Citizen

---

[6] Cf. Schopenhauer, pp. 430 and 518.

Wagner exempted himself on principle. Half unconsciously, he comes to terms with the impotence of the individual within the mechanism of the world as it exists. The gulf separating the individual who feels himself to be free and the all-embracing necessity in which he is enmeshed, is bridged by magic, but in a definitive manner, and the aesthetic insufficiency of the works— the over-motivation of the natural action—serves as the expression of a contradiction in which Wagner has acquiesced. The exoneration of the individual has its ideological function. Because he is unfree, he may do anything he wishes, since *sub specie aeternitatis* he is unable to wish for anything. The breach of the bourgeois norm is justified by its very absoluteness, without in any way impairing the moral integrity of the radiant heroes. When 'liberal' members of the bourgeoisie, the ageing Schopenhauer among them, waxed indignant about the adulteries of Siegmund and Tristan, this was not just out of sanctimony, but also from the certain realization that the Wagnerian semblance of freedom had contrived to pervert the bourgeois ideal into its antithesis. In the name of an allegedly higher necessity, the free man here is the stronger man who makes off with the property of the weak. To that extent even the bourgeois who ridicules King Mark is not completely absurd. The latter's willingness to forgive and forget, which is dressed up as the mellow wisdom and detachment of the man who has risen above a narrow-minded possessiveness, really implies the liberal's acceptance of defeat in the face of more modern methods. Mark is the ancestor of appeasement, who effectively glorifies violence by his 'wise' air of wonderment. The theory that the world is essentially evil redounds to the advantage of the world as it is. Wagner, the typical example of the late bourgeoisie, comes to resemble the early bourgeoisie, above all Hobbes, whom Schopenhauer was so fond of quoting.

In glorifying death by presenting it as ecstasy, Wagner deviates less radically than might be thought from Schopenhauer, his philosophical canon. Even though the latter conceives the transition to Nirvana in ascetic terms, elements of ecstasy are not alien to him. 'If, however, it should be absolutely insisted upon that in some way or other a positive knowledge should be attained of that which philosophy can only express negatively as the denial of the will, there would be nothing for it but to refer to that state, which all those who have attained to complete denial of the will have experienced, which has been variously denoted by the names ecstasy, rapture, illumination, union with God, and so forth; a state, however, which cannot properly be called knowledge, because it has not the form of subject and object, and is, moreover, only attainable in one's own experience and cannot be further communicated.'[7] In this passage Schopenhauer comes into conflict with his own fundamental doctrine—'But he who sees through the *principium individuationis,* and recognizes the real nature of the thing–in–itself, and thus the whole, is no longer susceptible of such consolation; he sees himself in all places at once, and withdraws. His will turns round, no longer asserts its own nature, which is reflected in the phenomenon, but denies it.'[8] The self-knowledge of the will, in its highest manifestation, is displaced once more by the unconscious, by ecstasy and that version of the *unio mystica* which is available on cheap offer in Wagner's works. Even in Schopenhauer there was a foretaste of the Wagnerian practice of dressing up death as salvation and of the inflated concept of the 'redeemer of the world'[9] which in Wagner becomes the ideo-logical climax of the entire oeuvre. In Schopenhauer the fallacy consists in the fact that the individual 'turning around' of the Will is sometimes thought of as gaining an ascendancy over the Will as a thing–in–itself, an ascendancy that strictly speaking does not follow logically from Schopenhauer's fundamental doctrine. For in theory the individual denial of life is supposed to be a matter of complete indifference to the Schopenhauerian Will, which would have to go on producing ever new suffering in accordance with the *principium individuationis* and without regard to the activities of the saints. With the concept of the redemption of the world, the particular reflective mind, the self-knowledge of the individual, contrives to smuggle in a speculative, substantive principle of the sort that Schopenhauer had repeatedly condemned in Hegel. The concept of redemption, born of the indifference of the conscious towards the unconscious, extends the ideology of pessimism to its

[7] Ibid., p. 536.
[8] Ibid. p. 498.
[9] Ibid., p. 477 et passim.

logical conclusion in Wagner. Under the title of redemption both
the negativity of the bourgeois world and its negation are deemed
equally positive. The destruction of the world at the end of the
Ring is also a Happy End. It adjusts itself to the scheme of death and
transfiguration which reveals its commodity character in the
phraseology of death notices, newspaper obituaries and tombstone
inscriptions. The very fact that death defies the imagination
becomes a means whereby to gild the badness of life. The category
of redemption is stripped of its theological meaning, but endowed
with the function of giving solace, without however acquiring any
precise content. It is a homecoming without a home, eternal rest
without Eternity, the mirage of peace without the underlying
reality of a human being to enjoy it. The reification of life extends
its domain even over death, since it ascribes to the dead the
happiness it withholds from the living. In exchange, it reserves for
itself its property rights over existence without which the title of
happiness is doomed to remain a lie and an obscenity. It could
almost be said that in the name of redemption the dead are cheated
of their lives twice over. At bottom, the end of *The Twilight of the
Gods* is not so very different from that of Gounod's *Faust*, which
Wagner rightly detested and in which Gretchen appears as an angel
floating above the rooftops of a medium-sized German town. Its
gigantic panorama has its model in the picture-postcard pink at the
end of the *Dutchman* and in the overture with which it shares the
plagal effect borrowed from church music. Wagnerian
redemption—its Bengal light dominates completely in countless
finales of Liszt's as well as in drawing-room music—is the ultimate
phantasmagoria. For true transcendence it substitutes the mirage of
the enduring upwards-soaring individual who vanishes into thin
air at the moment of his annihilation. Nothing could reconcile the
spectator with an apparent reconciliation but the perfection of that
manifest appearance itself, the element of a *promesse de bonheur* in a
situation of complete absurdity, in cheap fiction or a circus finale.
In the innermost core of Wagner's idea of redemption dwells
nothingness. It too is empty. Wagner's phantasmagoria is a mirage
because it is the manifestation of the null and void. And this defines
the impulse underlying Wagner's style. It is the attempt to conjure
up out of mere subjectivity a being superior to and with authority

over that subjectivity, just as if it were a being that could reflect something greater than itself. He thereby becomes one of the founders of Art Nouveau and has points of similarity with Ibsen, whose beliefs and convictions differ so radically from his. His iconic world resembles Ibsen's with its impotent and hence hollow symbols of unattainable meaning—the hero dying with vine leaves in his hair[10] or the pointless tower of the Masterbuilder. And like Ibsen's, it is chimerical in character. Empty nothingness itself takes shape in his works:

> Where I awoke—I did not stay:
> Yet where I stayed, I cannot say.
> I never saw the sun, nor saw I land nor people:
> And what I saw I cannot tell you.
> That place had been my home forever,
> My home for evermore:
> In the vast realm of Universal Night.[11]

Ultimately, the solution to the question of Wagner's nihilism depends on finding the solution to such configurations.

It may well be that the elevation of nothing to something in Wagner's works is primarily the index of an attitude that takes the process of identification with an oppressive and mutilating power to extremes, to the point where he can view his own destruction with equanimity. Underlying this posture is Schopenhauer's conviction that 'a reversed point of view, if it were possible for us, would reverse the signs and show the real for us as nothing, and that nothing as the real.'[12] Extreme though such a standpoint may be, it is not without a basis in philosophy. This lies in the belief that 'the conception of the nothing is essentially relative, and always refers to a definite something which it negates.'[13] Schopenhauer has resolved the old controversy about the absolute 'nihil negativum' and the relative 'nihil relativum' in favour of the latter. Like

[10] The reference is to *Hedda Gabler*. *Translator's note.*
[11] *Tristan*, Act III, sc. 1. Tristan speaks these words on regaining consciousness after he has been wounded by Melot. *Translator's note.*
[12] Ibid., p. 536.
[13] Ibid. p. 534.

Hegel, his antipode, he thinks of the nothing as only one aspect of the movement of being, which is the whole. Something of this is to be found in Wagner. The configurations of nothingness are more than just attempts to adorn the empty abyss. They try at the same time by defining the nothing to establish the boundary line between nothingness and something, and to use the concept of negativity to gain a purchase on a reality that was slipping between his fingers. Tristan's 'How could that vision leave me?', [14] which refers to the presentiment of nothingness as something, seizes hold of the moment in which a complete negativity perfects the chimera of utopia. It is the moment of awakening. The passage in Act III of *Tristan*, where the horn in the orchestra soars above the boundary separating nothingness and something to catch the echo of the shepherd's melancholy song as Tristan stirs—that passage will survive as long as the fundamental experiences of the bourgeois era can still be felt by human beings. Together with the other passage, the scene of Brünnhilde's awakening, it is evidence of that glimmering awareness without which the concept of nothingness, or so Wagner's music would have us believe, could not be conceived of. If compassion is reserved for animals, then this is a moment in which animals have a role to play. As the survivor of a bygone age, Brünnhilde's horse seems to effect the transition into an alert present. And that bygone age is, according to Schopenhauer, absolute nothingness. If Wagner nihilistically reduces history to nature, then for its part nature, that totality of which nothingness dialectically forms a partial moment, sets limits to nothingness. No nothingness is posited in Wagner that fails to promise a nature that survives it. It is as the sign of this undestroyed nature that the Rhine Maidens triumphantly bear the ring they have recovered back home into the depths. And it is the image of depth that provides the Wagnerian concept of nothingness with its contours. In the last years of his life he became increasingly preoccupied with the reflected, insubstantial, hopeless, hybrid creatures of the depths: the flower maidens, Goethe's Mignon, the Undinas and beings without a soul with whom he compared

[14] *Tristan*, ibid. The vision is of the Universal Night, mentioned above. *Translator's note.*

Cosima shortly before his death. They are the messengers from nothingness to existence and the profoundest intention of his music is to rescue them. In his Dresden period, Wagner had been friendly with Robert Reinick, the painter and poet. Perhaps he was acquainted with Reinick's fairy-story *The Island of Reeds*, which tells how a fisherman's daughter with the highly suggestive name of Hella[15] falls victim to the spell of a floating island and its childlike inhabitants. She is unable to escape from the charm of their songs and is finally swept away by the waters as she sings a song about a rock in a lake to the villagers who live on the shore. The song contains the lines,

> 'Tis time, 'tis time, on earth comes the night!
> Quick beneath the waves, for there it is light!

If Wagner's music undertakes the task of decoding the message of nothingness from the corrupt stock of allegorical images current in his age, then, conversely, the outlines of that void become utopian as the implied antithesis of the contours of his own age. On earth comes the night, but in the water it is light: the entire hatred and the dream-content of Wagner's work culminate in this Pythian gospel. We can hear like an echo in the final lines of the *Rhinegold* what the *Ring*, as the luminous facsimile of the great systems, could ultimately see in them: the senseless, jejune, hopeless and solitary hope that nothingness offers to the man who is tragically ensnared:

> Rhinegold! Rhinegold! Purest gold!
> If but your bright gleam still glittered in the deep!
> Now only in the depths is there tenderness and truth:
> False and faint-hearted are those who revel above![16]

As a refuge, these depths also conceal everything that the work 'falsely and faint-heartedly' betrayed. In the bad infinity of a society that reproduces itself aimlessly, the image of nature is distorted and compressed into that of the nothingness which becomes the only gap in an all-encompassing prison. At the same

[15] It suggests 'brightness', 'light', but also 'Hell'. *Translator's note.*
[16] *Rhinegold*, sc. 4.

time, however, that nothingness has a role to play in the service of the Hell that is mobilized to combat the deceptively coherent system of his works and society. In Act II of *The Valkyrie*, which really does stand in need of a terrorist God, sentence is passed on that system, on its idealization and even its destruction, to the effect that the work does not proclaim the need for submission to the edicts of fate. It is not Siegfried, but Siegmund, the hero dying without hope, who keeps faith with the dream of freedom. He rejects the heroic ideal that he embodies more truly than those well-established heroes who win the battle even before they start to fight. He refuses to follow Brünnhilde to Valhalla when the Absolute denies him the happiness of individuation that is libelled by Wagner and Schopenhauer alike:

> If I must die I shall not go to Valhalla.
> Let Hell hold me fast.[17]

Hell is the kingdom of Alberich, who sets out to storm Valhalla. This is the only place where to all intents and purposes justice is done to Valhalla; here alone does justice dwell. Not Schopenhauer's 'eternal' justice; rather the justice that does not escape from the circular track of red-hot coals, but authentically steps forth. It is this justice with which the story begins and which abolishes as prehistory that pre-conscious myth.

Wagner's works provide eloquent evidence of the early phase of bourgeois decadence. Within the framework of the parable, this impulse to destroy anticipates society's own destructiveness. It is in this rather than in any biological sense that Nietzsche's criticism of Wagner's decadence is legitimate. However, if a decadent society develops the seeds of the society that will perhaps one day take its place, then Nietzsche, like the Russian despotism of the twentieth century which followed him, failed to recognize the forces that were released in the early stages of bourgeois decline. There is not one decadent element in Wagner's work from which a productive mind could not extract the forces of the future. The weakening of the monad, which is no longer equal to its situation as monad and

[17] *The Valkyrie*, Act II, sc. 4.

which therefore sinks back passively beneath the pressure of the totality, is not just representative of a doomed society. It also releases the forces that had previously grown up within itself, thus turning the monad into the 'phenomenal being' as conceived of by Schopenhauer. There is more of the social process in the limp individuality of Wagner's work than in aesthetic personas more equal to the challenge posed by society and hence more resolute in meeting it. Even the masochistic capitulation of the ego is more than just masochistic. It is doubtless true that subjectivity surrenders its happiness to death; but by the same token it acknowledges a dawning realization that it does not wholly belong to itself. The monad is 'sick', it is too impotent to enable its principle, that of isolated singularity, to prevail and to endure. It therefore surrenders itself. Its capitulation, however, does more than just help an evil society to victory over its own protest. Ultimately it also smashes through the foundations of the evil isolation of the individual himself. To die in love means also to become conscious of the limits imposed on the power of the property system over man. It means also to discover that the claims of pleasure, where they were followed through, would burst asunder that concept of the person as an autonomous, self-possessed being that degrades its own life to that of a thing, and which deludes itself into believing that it will find pleasure in the full possession of itself, whereas in reality that pleasure is frustrated by the fact of self-possession. It is true that Siegfried is too tight-fisted to return the ring to the Rhine Maidens. But at the moment when he ensures that his own self-deception will be complete, he finds the gesture of throwing behind him the clod of earth which stands for the individual life that a man need not cling to once he has received what it has promised. [18]

Hence, Wagner is not only the willing prophet and diligent lackey of imperialism and late-bourgeois terrorism. He also possesses the neurotic's ability to contemplate his own decadence and to transcend it in an image that can withstand that all-consuming gaze. It might well be asked whether Nietzsche's

[18] See *The Twilight of the Gods*, Act III, sc. 1: 'For life and limb, /see—thus I fling them from me!' (He picks up the clod of earth, holds it above his head and on his last words throws it behind him.) *Translator's note.*

criterion of health is of greater benefit than the critical consciousness that Wagner's grandiose weakness acquires in his commerce
with the unconscious forces responsible for his own decadence. As
he falls, he gains possession of himself. His consciousness is
schooled in the night that threatens to overwhelm consciousness.
The imperialist dreams of the catastrophic end of imperialism; the
bourgeois nihilist sees through the nihilism of the age that will
follow his own. At the end of the late essay, 'Art and Revolution',
we read: 'it can but arouse our apprehension to see the progress of the
art of war departing from the springs of moral force, and turning
more and more to the mechanical: here the rawest forces of the
lower powers of nature are brought into an artificial play, in
which, for all arithmetic and mathematics, the blind Will might
one day break its leash and intervene with elemental force. Already
a grim and ghostly sight is offered by the armoured Monitors,[19]
against which the stately sailing-ship avails no more: dumb
serving-men no longer with the looks of men attend these
monsters, nor even will they desert from their awful boiler-rooms.
But just as in Nature everything has its destroying foe, so Art
invents torpedoes for the sea, and dynamite cartouches, or the like,
for everywhere else. It is conceivable —that all of this, with art and
science, valour, point of honour, life and chattels, might one day
fly into the air through some incalculable accident.'[20] But
Wagner's music knows more about this than do his words.
Through a twist of the dialectic, music is transformed from the
companion of the unconscious into the first conscious companion:
the first that knowledge commands and which can be set to work
by knowledge for its purposes. Despite all this, Wagner not
unjustifiably preferred to compare himself to the interpreter of
dreams rather than to the dreamer. But to interpret the dream one
must be both weak and strong enough to surrender oneself to the
dream without reserve. In *Tristan* we find more than the rapturous
music of dream and death, more than the delights of the

[19] A Monitor was a low-lying iron-clad ship with revolving gun-turrets; it
takes its name from the first American ship of its kind, built in 1862. *Translator's
note.*

[20] *Richard Wagner's Prose Works*, Vol. 6, *Religion and Art*, New York 1966,
p. 252.

unconscious which in reality has never 'been cooled by atonement', because, as an unfree and unconscious delight, it is as
unattainable as all pleasure in Schopenhauer's philosophy and
hence disguises itself in atonement. The feverish passages in Act III
of *Tristan* contain that black, abrupt, jagged music which instead
of underlining the vision unmasks it. Music, the most magical of all
the arts, learns how to break the spell it casts over the characters.
When Tristan curses love, this is more than the impotent sacrifice
offered up by rapture to asceticism. It is the rebellion—futile
though it may be—of the music against the iron laws that rule it,
and only in its total determination by those laws can it regain the
power of self-determination. It is not for nothing that those phrases
in the *Tristan* score which follow the words '*Der furchtbare Trank*'
['that potion so dread'] stand on the threshold of modern music in
whose first canonic work, Schoenberg's F# minor quartet, we
find the words, 'Nimm mir die Liebe, gib mir dein Glück!'[21] They
mean that love and happiness are false in the world in which we
live, and that the whole power of love has passed over into its
antithesis. Anyone able to snatch such gold from the deafening
surge of the Wagnerian orchestra, would be rewarded by its
altered sound, for it would grant him that solace which, for all its
rapture and phantasmagoria, it consistently refuses. By voicing the
fears of helpless people, it could signal help for the helpless,
however feebly and distortedly. In doing so it would renew the
promise contained in the age-old protest of music: the promise of a
life without fear.

[21] 'Take love from me, give me your happiness!' These words are taken from
Stefan George's poem 'Litany'. *Translator's note.*

Index

The name of Richard Wagner has been omitted from the index.

Musical Works by Wagner

General Index

So long, Time & Deviation

99 - music - memory
103-A - music & long

33
c46/
60
63
83
Spaced 86
87
88 - cb Bulo?
(91 - time, eternity)

Chapter 3 - alles — 100
55. long - all - wire met
85 - arth. generally

124. underworld
119 - bad rch — v d
— 752. topic

Apthegm